LEGENDARY!

How Any Student Can Become a Legendary Leader!

Lamarr Womble with Jono Croskey

CoolSpeak Publishing Company
Copyright © 2023 Lamarr Womble
All rights reserved.

ISBN-13: 979-8-218-17620-4

Table of Contents

An Introduction - Where Legends Are Made!

I'm Lamarr Womble and just about everyone who knew me in college would probably say, "Everyone knows Lamarr!"

If someone didn't know me, others might say, "How do you not know Lamarr?"

When I look back at those college years, I wonder what that person thought when someone asked that. *'How do you not know Lamarr?'* My name was everywhere, but it wasn't because I'm so great. It was because I *wanted* it to be.

The experiences, connections and learning outside the classroom I had in college helped me build my future. They all helped me become **legendary**.

Two years after I graduated in 2006, I launched **Passion for Leadership,** my motivational speaking and education consulting company that focuses on school culture and climate, developing positive student mindsets, student leadership development, and helping young people go after their passions! I've spoken to over 60,000 students and educators since 2008.

In 2013, I moved to New York City to become a **Dream Director** for The Future Project. I specifically helped students build projects based on their passions and dreams. Since then, I've developed hundreds of student leaders, supported them to make impactful change and individually coached them through mental and life challenges. So much of my life (to this point) is directly related to who I was in college and was enhanced by developing young leaders.

It's from these experiences over the last 20 years that I wrote this book … so you, too, can become a legend!

In the summer of 2001, I started my college career at the University of Nebraska Omaha. The experience was kicked off with the new student orientation. In June, prior to orientation, I was your typical high school senior; I didn't really have a clue about college.

All students know that when you don't have a clue, you just rely on your mom to do everything. Let's be honest, moms always have a clue; it's what they do!

I don't remember much about preparing for college because it wasn't emphasized in high school then as much as it is now. The one thing I remember is deciding between the University of Nebraska-Omaha and the University of Nebraska-Lincoln because my parents were getting ready to move to Las Vegas. I never visited Nebraska-Lincoln but was considering it because they had residence halls.

At the time, UNO had just built residence halls on their campus three years earlier. My decision came that summer, right before 9/11. My parents were having trouble selling their house. My dad left for Las Vegas in July and my mom stuck around to try and sell the house and continue applying for transfers within her company to Las Vegas. At that point, I decided to stay at home and commute to the University of Nebraska-Omaha. The bottom line was it didn't matter where I went to college; I just knew I had to go. Mom said so!

Once I committed to the school, I made a decision, even before heading out to orientation. I was going to meet as many people who didn't go to Bellevue West High School as I could. In 2001, UNO was just beginning to shed its "commuter campus" reputation and everyone thought if you went to school there it was going to be exactly like high school. Since I didn't have a clue about the school's reputation at that time, I went in with the complete opposite attitude.

It would be that attitude that allowed me to walk into the new student orientation not knowing a soul and walking out enjoying connections with other students I thought would carry over into the fall ... when school started.

Growing up in Bellevue, Nebraska, a suburb of Omaha, I never really met anyone from outside of the area. I was oblivious to the fact that there were so many kids coming to UNO from all over the state.

The first two kids I met were from Hastings. What? Hastings, you ask? Where is that? That's what I thought.

Conrad and Austin Parks were fraternal twins from the place where Kool-Aid originated. I bet you had no idea that the most stereotyped drink in America was started in one of the whitest towns in the country. I'm not sure why I connected with these two guys right away. At face value they were the *least* likely of anybody at orientation I would have assumed I'd connect with. It might have been because the three of us were the most obnoxious. We exuded confidence.

I like to simply call us "fun-havers" or "social butterflies" or even "party starters."

It didn't hurt that they were coming to UNO to play football. Maybe I thought if I could align myself with some football players I'd meet more people. Either way, the connection was made.

I knew when I got back to campus in the fall that they would be the first dudes I'd seek out. At the end of orientation I was excited about the new friendships I made, but I wasn't necessarily excited about college.

I also made another decision that day. I wanted to be an **Orientation Leader** someday. When I made that decision, I had no idea it would lead me down the path it did. I didn't know *how* to become an orientation leader or if I was even good enough to do the job. As a result, it was a path that would allow me to become **LEGEN** … wait for it … **DARY**!

It was the first of many jobs on UNO's campus that allowed me to develop specific skills and establish a leadership track that would provide a wealth of experience, numerous long-term friendships, long-term professional networks and a personal brand that would last well after college and eventually turn into a business.

My job as an Orientation Leader would lead me to meet my social match, the Batman to my Robin, the Jordan to my Pippen. I met Jono Croskey. He was a fast talkin', fast walkin', always partyin' guy, and he was also a leading guy from Omaha Central High School who transferred back to UNO after a short stint at the University of Nebraska Kearney.

Oddly enough, while Jono and I were still in high school, we were rivals before we ever knew each other. It was always Bellevue West vs. Omaha Central. Go T-BIRDS! Despite that, we became fast friends with similar experiences from two very different high schools. Ultimately, we were on a collision course to meet at UNO and I'm glad we did.

Jono and I discussed writing this book for years so we could share our experiences, but more importantly, to share the stories of other campus legends. As I sit and think about what our experiences were, **I never had any intention of becoming a legend on my campus**.

It just happened.

Lots of folks would claim it was because I talked to everyone. I did. But I can recall students who attended UNO while Jono and I were there and who were nowhere near as social as we were but were just as legendary. People like Steve Massara and Elizabeth Kraemer left indelible footprints on our campus.

Jono and I reconnecting in 2022 in California.

The point is there are many factors that lead a person to become **legendary**. Leadership styles, personalities, drive and determination, and so on can all help students become Legendary. In this book we're going to spend time exploring what those traits are and answer questions about what it takes to become Legendary so that any student -no matter who they are, where they come from or what college or university they choose- can become

Legendary! Even if you decide not to go to college; these Legendary lessons can work in any workplace.

This book will provide the roadmap to be **Legen** … wait for it … **DARY**!

So, what is legendary status?

In our opinion, it means three things:

1) Students, faculty and staff still talk about you on campus to this day because of the massive footprint you left behind. Maybe it's because you started or led an amazing club. Maybe it's because you threw some memorable parties. Maybe it's the care and concern you showed everyone on your campus. Whatever "IT" is, it's all part of a larger formula that helps you become legendary!

2) If we were to ask anyone from your campus who graduated a year before you or a year after, "Who was *"That Person"* on campus while you went to school," if they can answer with your name, then you're in serious contention for LEGENDARY STATUS.

3) You begin to recognize that the leadership qualities, mentality and work habits you develop as a student leader are surely to follow you into your professional career no matter what you do. These are the skills that will separate you from the rest of the pack!

There's something that makes us remember the EPIC ones. There really is an aura about that person almost everyone holds in high regard. This counts for those in college and out.

Who is the person in your life who makes you smile the most, calms you down the fastest, gets your humor the best, or is always there for you? I believe legends embody all of these things through social, leadership, and academic success.

It's not being looked at as legends that makes them special but what they do to impact every person they come in contact with that causes people to say their name as an answer to every question we just asked.

That's what this is about. So ask yourself, "Do you want to be LEGEN ... wait for it ... DARY?"

Let's rock!

Legendary Lesson 1: How to BE a People PERSON!

1.1. What's your "people" philosophy?

As I matured through college, I realized the importance of relationships in leadership. People will follow you anywhere you're trying to lead them *if* they know you genuinely care about them and their well-being. This goes for their personal and professional life, including success at school or work.

Some folks like to draw a hard line between personal and professional, but the more blurred the lines, the more impact leaders can have on the relationships around them. Respect boundaries and meet your people where they are. Go deeper from there, it starts with respect.

In my keynote speeches, I often end by saying, 'If you want to be a great leader, start by just being a great person.'

Be 'others' centered.

Use language like *us, we, the group, the team, the family*. Once you've mastered that, you then need to be someone who **executes**.

If you can be Others-Centered and execute on you and your team's ideas, you will be LEGENDARY. This is the basics of leadership.

If you want to be LEGEN … wait for it … DARY, you have to possess a "people philosophy." You need to determine how you want to interact with every student there, if at all. How are you going to approach them, speak to them, make them feel memorable, help them find their way, help them feel better about themselves on the day when it seems like they're in the dumps?

Everyone who desires to be Legendary doesn't have to be an extreme extrovert like Jono and I were. If you care about leadership, you *must* care about people, so even as an introvert, you have to develop a people philosophy.

Introverted leaders, your superpower is in the one-on-one relationship. This is where you shine because you have the opportunity to **listen** and **hear** the people you lead and interact with. Introverted legends are typically those who hear what's being said or communicated without it having to be verbally spoken. Introverts pick up on body language, temperament, and language to recognize ways to make an impact on a person's life. Introverted legends are thoughtful and empathetic.

Your "people philosophy" will lead to social and leadership capital. Now, I'm using the term "Social Capital" and "Leadership Capital" in the same way one might talk about political capital. This type of capital is about **building** relationships, trust, and support you can rely on when you need it in the future.

How can you create such great relationships with the general population on your campus? How can the specific population of people you lead or impact be willing to do things for you they would not do for others? What access can you be allowed that others cannot attain? In what ways will your organization-centered ideas be taken seriously and not just brushed aside as talk instead of action? What do you want your legacy to be with everyone you interact with? That's **capital**.

My "people philosophy" is this: **"I want to help people discover their passions and live a happier life based on their own definition of what success means!"**

Your people philosophy isn't just how you want to leave people. It's an accountability check for you to live up to and into the person you say you want to be each day!

Take a few minutes, think about this deeply, and write your people philosophy. It can be a saying you already live by, a quote, a song lyric, or anything that displays how you want to treat people.

Write it here:

PEOPLE PHILOSOPHY

1.2 Remember names like it's your JOB!

It basically *is* your job, especially when you first move to campus as a freshmen and **especially** during your first two weeks. Remember **everyone's** name!

This may have been the one thing that proved to be the most powerful for Jono and me during our tenure at UNO. This created unbelievable social capital between the entire student body and us.

It showed that we cared enough to introduce ourselves and remember a person's name the next time we saw them. And it carried a lot of weight.

When you do this, it shows that you're an **effective listener**. But so many times when you meet people, the most important part of the conversation goes in one ear and out the other: THE INTRODUCTION and THEIR NAME!

Bill Clinton was on MSNBC in 2013 talking about his childhood. He shared a story about how his mother taught him the importance of remembering people's names because of how it can make people feel. As a politician, he also benefited from that skill.

LEGENDARY Leaders, I cannot stress enough how important it is for you to build relationships on your campuses and within your organizations. You should know everyone's name. When you get down to it, most names are about one to two syllables. At most. It's not hard to remember … *if* you care. And if you care, it shows. So, try harder.

I realize you're still in high school or (just starting) college and it can be very dramatic sometimes or some people can appear unable to relate to you, but just remembering their name makes a difference. It affects people.

If you've ever seen the movie, *What Women Want*, starring Mel Gibson, you can relate: there's a scene where Mel Gibson's character actually recognizes the intern who did his ad work, and it changed her world. This is the kind of impact you'll have by simply remembering names. When you have a lot of status, you can guarantee someone is going to feel like they're invisible to you.

Don't let this happen. *See* people.

Your name is how people identify you to the entire world. Your name may be said millions of times in your lifetime. Just think about that; that's how important it is. If people know your name, think about how easy it is to start a conversation as opposed to when they don't.

Or consider times when you run into somebody you met, but can't recall their name. How does that make them feel? How do *you* feel when someone doesn't (or won't) remember yours? We need to be empathetic and see things from every perspective and when we do, we realize how valuable the simple and free act of remembering names becomes.

During hostage situations, want to know what the negotiators do first? Establish a connection to the hostage-taker. They ask his or her name. Then they use it *constantly*. *If* they find out one of the victims' names, they'll repeat that over and over, too. Why? Because a person with a name **matters**! That's why. And if you get in the habit of remembering people's names, they'll connect with you *more* because you make them feel as though *they matter!*

Oftentimes, I think about how people answer phones at businesses or retail locations. When employees answer the phone and say, "Hello, this is Michelle," think about how much easier it is to dive into a conversation explaining why you're calling as opposed to someone who doesn't state their name at the beginning. Also, think about how that person feels when you address them by their name. They tend to go the extra mile to help whereas they may only do the minimal for those who never bother to listen.

In college, Jono and I met tons of new students every summer as Orientation Leaders. Orientation made it easy because they all wore name tags. Where Jono and I made connections for life, gained lots of respect and were able to lead other students is when we got back to campus that fall and *still* remembered their names. Keep in mind, this was pre-social media!

In moments like that, I knew that every person who had that type of experience with Jono and me were going to be extremely loyal, appreciative and even trusting of our leadership ability.

There was one particular instance I remember completely shocking a group of people by remembering their names. I was heading to an off-campus party hosted by a friend of mine. When I walked in, there were three people I met a few months earlier who just happened to be at the same party. I walked right up to them after giving them the 'head nod.' I said, "I remember you guys, let me try to remember your names." I nailed them all: Tracy, Jared and Chris!

One of my favorite authors, Gary Vaynerchuk, often refers to a generation when you walked into the butcher shop for your meat, the butcher already knew your name and what you wanted as soon as you stepped through the door. All the butcher would do was greet you, wrap your meat and send you on your way. When I think about building relationships through names and using that in leadership, I think of the same exact scenario.

Students on your campus or high school should walk into your office, room or space and you should know who they are and address them by their name. They should say things like, "Oh, you remembered my name?" Or, "How do you even know my name?" Or, "Wow, you remembered who I am." Or, "You remember names well!"

Often, those types of statements make me feel good about myself knowing that I did remember. Everyone should be working on becoming the butcher and creating relationships by getting to know people *personally*.

Your name is how you identify with the world. Think about how critical it is that you know someone else's name, especially during the first couple of times you meet them.

It says a lot about who you are. It says a lot about the listener you are, the care you have to **value** others. In too many cases, it's socially acceptable to not remember names right away. Most people don't expect you to remember because the standard for themselves is the same.

As a Legendary Leader on campus or at work, I'm asking you to change the status quo. Change the minimum expectation because, if you do, everyone else will value the same sentiments and push this type of relationship building message.

In most cases, when you forget, you'll probably reintroduce yourself, but then you forget again and don't care anymore, right? Jono and I are asking you to create opportunities to be endeared by the ones who follow you. Remembering faces isn't good enough; how are you making people feel when you say, 'I remember your face but I can't remember your name'?

This is what they hear: *I wasn't listening or didn't care to remember your name in the first place.*

Tips and Opportunities to Practice Remembering Names:

1) Start by caring to learn people's names and **try harder**.

2) When you meet someone at a networking event or even just casually while out with friends, ask their name once at the beginning of the conversation, then again at the end of it; if you forget, just ask for their name again.

3) Social Media is great for helping you remember names. The power of having a personal database with everyone you've ever met over the last 10 years is powerful. Our advice: friend everybody in person and online!

4) The use of a nickname is awesome! If you ask a room of 30 people if they have a nickname, I can bet that 20-25 students have one. Nicknames are great because they *mean something*. Typically, they come from family and friends and people we care about the most. People will sometimes introduce themselves as their nickname. Use it.

5) Traveling on a plane? Practice asking names right from the beginning. In most scenarios on a plane, train or bus you can sit and have an entire conversation without ever asking the person's name, but get in the habit of starting conversations by sharing your name. Most people will then share theirs.

6) At a Leadership Conference? Use the name tag consistently to help you (no brainer), but the person who impresses the most is the one who remembers without having to look.

7) When answering the phone in your organization's space or unidentified numbers on your personal cell, answer with your name.

8) At a restaurant or store working with a customer service representative, be sure to use their name when you address them. Also, use their name a few times throughout the conversation.

1.3 How to DO YOU and be a team player!

Self Awareness & Perception.

How do you project yourself to the world? How do people perceive you? Are you *never* serious? Are you socially awkward? Do you know when to step back and let others lead or do you keep pressing forward to lead? Do you recognize when you're being pushy? Do you know when you need support? Are you closed off to the world? Are you a complainer?

Self-awareness is challenging because it really is an evaluation of yourself and the person you've become as you graduate high school and college. Evaluation of yourself is directly related to self-esteem, usually of your physical presence. But this is all about your **mental self-esteem**. You can either self-evaluate or (what's more effective) ask your closest friends to keep you in check to make you aware of how you project in all situations.

Ask 5 people these self evaluation questions:

1) What are some of my best qualities?
2) What are some qualities I need to work on?
3) How do I show up as a leader?
4) How can I improve our relationship?
5) Am I accountable for my words and actions?

Consistently being aware of how you project yourself to the world is pivotal in creating a personal brand on campus.

One of my first jobs out of college was working for a non-profit called INROADS that helped minority students prepare for corporate interviews and internship opportunities. I was a National Recruiter and remember how my boss, Andre Lee, would always respond the same way when anyone asked how his day was. He would respond by saying, "Loving every minute of it!"

I asked him why he did that. He said, "No matter what's going on in your life or in the lives of others, people need to know that you're a steady and self-aware leader."

I realized that answering that question negatively has influence on how people view you. If you always answer, "It's okay" or, "I'm alright," over time it drains the energy out of people and you may not even realize you're doing it. As a leader, you may not realize that people are beginning to subconsciously form an opinion about you, which impacts your ability to lead.

The idea of repetition building personal brand recognition is influential and just as it could come off negatively, it could come off positively just as easily and take you to new heights as a leader or collaborator of people within your organization. It's not that you can't have your moments of being in a bad mood. But as the leader you have to have a system to vent and get negative feelings off of your chest. Journaling or a trusted mentor or advisor what I'd recommend.

Make Someone's Day.

Jono could talk to you all day about making someone's day. I honestly believe it was the common thread that connected Jono and me (besides our over-the-top social personalities). When we began talking about writing this book, one of the first things that came up was *why* we would do it.

Jono told me there was nothing better for him on a day-to-day basis than making someone else feel incredible about themselves. For me, I was also motivated by the opportunity to make people on UNO's campus feel great about themselves!

I was more interested in the ability to notice human beings and pay attention to all the people around me. At some level, I was a 'creeper.' I noticed everything I could about people. Jono was also quite skilled at this.

We noticed the new haircut, a new outfit, her new shoes, maybe when he needed an emotional pick-me-up, when someone needed a laugh. Jono and I always set out to be those guys. It was never about popularity; it was building personal brand capital socially, academically and value for ourselves.

We are giving you permission to be the biggest creepers on your whole campus because noticing sparks conversation, conversation sparks common interests, common interests spark truly connecting, truly connecting sparks friendships, friendships ensure that on your campus everyone knows you are sincerely looking out for the well-being of each person you meet. Even if they don't know you, they should have heard about you or there should be rumblings about the type of person you are on campus or at work.

So, how do your friends and others introduce you?

At the very beginning of this book I mentioned that people would introduce Jono and me to new people all the time. Often, people we'd never met before but may have seen in the past or at least recognized, we paid attention to them, too. The person doing the introducing would always ask, "How do you not know Jono and Lamarr? They know everybody!"

I never really analyzed these conversations until recently when I learned that some people thought I was arrogant. It was part of the reason that influenced us to write this book. It made me wonder what the other person was thinking when someone introduced us and literally made us sound like the coolest dudes on the planet or as LEGENDS in the making. In retrospect, I would have thought to myself, "Well dang, why don't I know these guys?" These conversations even happened when we weren't around. The legend grows. These types of conversations *still* happen.

Oh the irony, a legend is a folk story, made up, someone created it *for* you, about you and oftentimes without you. That mystery actually made us *more* legendary than we probably were, but our legendary status was never self-proclaimed, it was created by the people we interacted with on a daily basis. That's the **secret** to being legendary … you can't force it upon others. If you try, you'll become notorious (and if you don't know the meaning of that word, look it up) … and that's not what you want.

The reality is that all through college I remained close with my high school friends, none of whom went to UNO for more than a year before they transferred elsewhere.

During college, I was with Jose, Dustin, Travis, Mishari and Jono. My closest friends never changed throughout my whole college experience. If I was that arrogant, typically your closest friends will be the first to tell you or at least notice if you were acting like you're all that and a bag of chips.

I'm very confident that none of them had any reason to offer advice about how I got "too good" for them throughout the years. That's because I didn't.

As my legend grew, they grew with me. They preferred my legend, actually. They knew when it came down to it, when they were visiting me, it was going to be a good time. When you know where the party is and your crew has connections to any number of different groups of people, other crews, legends can build even quicker. This is exactly what happened with Jono, Jose, Mishari, and me!

Even with the ladies (and this is unconfirmed, but let's be real) -in high school and college- many girls and guys tend to want to be affiliated with the who's who on campus. Ironically, that was never really my style, which is exactly why my closest friends remained the same. The best part was going to visit my friends on their campuses and recognizing their legendary status as an outsider on their turf!

So, how are you being introduced?

Legendary Lesson 2 – How to Build Your Personal Brand

2.1 What is a brand?

A brand, simply put, is an entity that's often recognized by a symbol, a logo, a name or sound/song, a phrase or a picture. Branding is the promotion of these things to create a positive image in your mind about what they represent.

The best brands in the world are easily recognizable. Consider (and fill in the blanks):

1) Just Do it! _____ Their logo is _____
2) The Few, The Proud, The _____
3) Beats By _____. Their logo is a _____.
4) Mac vs PC, which is _____ vs _____
5) The Worldwide Leader in Sports is _____

When people think of your campus, the next thing they should think of is YOU!

With the emergence of the Internet and the ability to have access to creating your own platform, it set the stage for individuals to be superstars on the web. In terms of how this relates to a college campus, you have the same ability to create a brand on campus in-person as you do online.

When I was coming to college in 2001, I had every intention of meeting as many people as I could and this was *before* social media and websites like Facebook that made it much easier to stay connected to the people you meet. If Facebook was around from the start of my college career, who knows the social impact I could have had from 2001 to 2005 (before I actually got signed up on that platform).

A personal brand is defined as the practice of people marketing themselves and their careers. In other words, with a personal brand, you **are** the brand. This includes *all* of your social media platforms, specifically LinkedIn, Instagram, TikTok and Twitter. Here you have the opportunity to gain followers, meet more people and push a message that is specific to your brand or however you want to make yourself known on campus.

College campuses are the perfect place to start a revolution of some kind. This is where a personal brand or an organization's brand gets built and things get crazy. Students are always looking for something or someone to latch onto who's **daring to be different** and creative in order to change the status quo.

This becomes very important in creating a **legendary** status on campus. It doesn't matter what you create; if you're affiliated with something that's catchy, fun, and original, it could be something that follows you throughout your college career … and that's a good thing.

2.2. How to make the most of your Social Media Platforms

If you're looking to build a personal brand on campus these days, the answer is simple: you need to be on **five** main platforms: YouTube, TikTok, Twitter, Instagram, and LinkedIn. Twitter is still relevant to brand building, but much less now than three or four years ago because of the emergence of Instagram and how much more personal pictures allow you to be with your life (and your followers/connections).

In so many ways, Instagram has become the more personal Twitter (not because of the content you share because the content is always personal) but based on who you allow to follow you. Twitter is the ultimate follow-anybody-and-anybody-can-follow-you platform. Facebook is the 'I am only going to send you a friend request if I know you and want you to know my business' platform.

Instagram has become the ultimate hybrid between the two, which allows you to share very personal experiences with the world and we, oddly enough, do not care who is following us and I know for the students I work with in high school, the more followers, the better. But if it was Facebook and someone you didn't know who sent you a request and you've never met them, you would think twice or deny that request.

There was a time when Facebook was the ultimate college personal branding and marketing tool because there was a time (yes, there was a time) when Facebook was only available to college and university students. That's how it started! We know that exclusivity into any group makes it more appealing and mysterious to many folks who want to learn or be a part of something they may not be bold enough to start or create themselves.

The awesome thing about Facebook is that you can still be a branding rockstar on it because in the world we live in (through social media), perception is reality. Although students are heavily focused on TikTok, Instagram or Snapchat, Facebook is still the place to initiate and make long-term connections with people you meet on campus. Remember, I said 'connections.' There's a difference!

For athletes and HS students who plan to prep their social media pages (unless they're building a separate brand)"

THE IDEAL SOCIAL MEDIA PROFILE FOR STUDENT LEADERS/ATHLETES

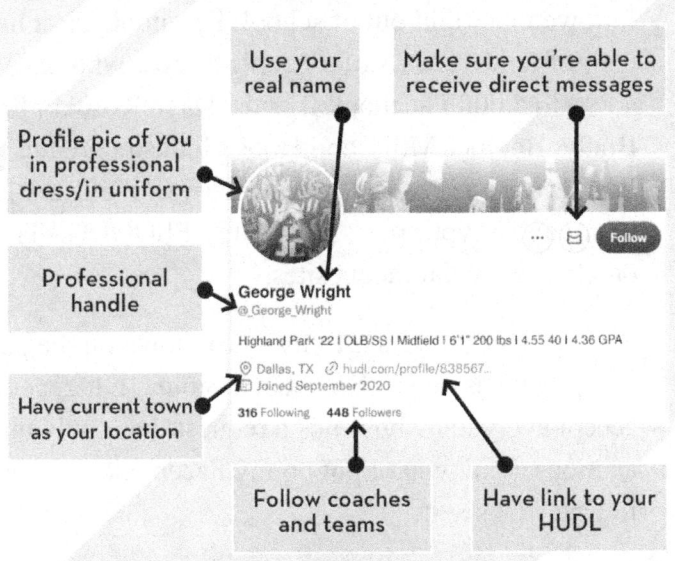

Use your real name

Make sure you're able to receive direct messages

Profile pic of you in professional dress/in uniform

Professional handle

Have current town as your location

Follow coaches and teams

Have link to your HUDL

George Wright
@_George_Wright

Highland Park '22 | OLB/SS | Midfield | 6'1" 200 lbs | 4.55 40 | 4.36 GPA

⊙ Dallas, TX   ⊘ hudl.com/profile/838567...
☐ Joined September 2020

316 Following   **448** Followers

IMPORTANT

When you "like" something, you're telling the world you endorse that, which colleges and coaches can see. Be careful what you like.

BIO SHOULD HAVE

- High school (spell it out)
- GPA (ACT/SAT scores also good)
- C/O (class of) 2022, 2023, etc.
- Your position
- Other sports and organizations
- Height / weight
- Limit use of emojis in bio
- Ranking from 247, rivals, ESPN, etc.

Remember, you won't be in college forever.

LinkedIn is the place for students to seek out internships and jobs after college, which requires you to build your LinkedIn pages *while* you're in school. When I was close to graduating college in 2006, I was a Facebook superstar and that perception of "knowing everybody" followed me right out of school. Facebook has a limit of 5,000 friends. I am 1 of 5 people I know who have between 4,800 to 5,000 Facebook friends. Dayo Kosoko, Frank Brady, Boomer Mills, and Hook Hookstra are the others. Brands are built based on how many eyeballs are following your page or your posts. LET THE FLOODGATES OPEN on **all** your social media sites.

Over the years, I've slowed down on the pace that I accept friends on my Facebook account, but generally I still accept everyone who sends a request. I am only more cautious about what I put on my Facebook page as opposed to who I let see it.

For myself, my growing influence among youth requires me to be smarter about what I post but I also keep it entirely real so students know what I'm about. I rarely post personal things on my social media now. I post things promoting my business and my brand and that's a boundary that helps me stay focused on not worrying about keeping up with everyone else on social media. If you're a "private person," that's fine. Be choosy. Draw a boundary between your life and social media. But if you're trying to build a brand, DOCUMENTING > CREATING. This way you don't have to worry about creating; you end up just documenting everything you're doing.

What about those friends you have who say they're taking a "break" from social media? When you're building a personal brand on campus to become **legendary**, there's no time for breaks. Friend everyone, all the time. Better yet, let them friend you. The more people who have access to your world, the more influential you can be in pushing whatever revolution you're trying to start.

This is the new normal. There are a number of young people who have built massive personal brands on TikTok, YouTube, Instagram, Snapchat and Twitter and have gained notoriety because of their social media presence. There's money to be made that can potentially be very connected to your passion.

Just like with business, being personal on a social media platform is beneficial, just like creating industry-based usernames that will require folks to start following up based on that topic or industry. Especially if you can be very witty.

For example, Scott Hinkle, who was a former student leader at the University of Nebraska Omaha and current graduate student at the University of Iowa started a Twitter account after his first term as student body president, which was called 2Termz. It was a clear play on hip hop artist 2Chainz's stage name. Although Scott was not allowed to run for a 2nd term, it seemed the account picked up steam and he was able to send out a number of tweets from this account recommending that he should be able to run for another term.

If you want to learn or improve your social media skills, I would recommend reading any book by social media guru Gary Vaynerchuk. They are fun reads that teach you very specific skills on developing passion and help you take your passions on campus and in your life and turn them into a personal brand or business you could build on campus. I would recommend *Crush It: Why now is the time to cash in on your people*. I would also recommend (specifically for social media), *Jab, Jab, Jab, Right Hook* which specifically talks about social media strategies that can help your brand.

2.3 How a nickname can help build your brand

If you want to be memorable on campus, if you want to be a living legend wherever you go, you *have* to be willing to have a nickname. I don't care if this nickname was given to you when you were younger or if you don't get one until you go to college: nicknames are one of the sure-fire ways to build a brand on campus.

This goes both ways; having a nickname but also consistently using someone else's nickname or coming up with a personal nickname for them. That will allow you to remember them easier (for the next time you meet or see them on campus).

I never really had a nickname that stuck *until* I got to college and created my own.

When I was younger, people would call me Urkel, Professor Fish, or Lame-mar. It wasn't until college when I decided to take control of my nickname and it stuck. So, in 2003, I became a resident assistant at the University of Nebraska-Omaha at Scott Village. These were the newest sets of residence halls at the university at the time and I was one of the inaugural RA's. Right around move-in, in August, PDiddy -one of my idols- had a huge show on MTV called "Making the Band" and Mase also on Bad Boy records at the time had returned from his hiatus from rapping and dropped the single, "Welcome Back." As RAs, we were always looking for creative ways to engage the students in our buildings, make people feel comfortable and get them excited about moving back in for the new school year to begin.

One night, I was working in the Scott Village residential office when it hit me! I would have my own version of Diddy's show "Making the Band," except my move-in theme would be "Making the Building." And I, of course, would be LDiddy! I was so excited about that whole idea I got to work right away preparing my materials for moving in.

LDiddy has stuck with me to this day. I even use it when I'm out speaking around the country. I give students a choice to call me Lamarr or LDiddy. LDiddy usually wins. This nickname has been yelled countless times in the streets of Omaha, but also on the campus of UNO.

Anybody who knew me then, including my residents who moved into building D that year will still call me LDiddy! The best part was when students moved in I played Mase's song "Welcome Back" which couldn't have been any more perfect. I still get excited when I think about how clever that was.

The point is that nicknames are fun, easy and memorable and they will help you become legendary. One thing that has always stuck with me about Jono and me (I mentioned this in the intro) is that he also had a nickname. Jono made up his own and whenever you would meet him he would say, "I'm Jono Croskey, that's right!" It became his whole name and nickname. Jono was obsessed with St. Louis Cardinals baseball and St. Louis in general so, by default, he had a man crush on Nelly the rapper at the time.

What are some of the greatest college nicknames of all time? We went on a search for them.

Dayo "Party All The Time" Kososko, Matthew "Hook" Hooker, Frank "Mr. Wonderful" Brady, Jason "J-Bomb" Blohm. Even my nickname has gone down in history; LDiddy, that's right. These are just a few that I know of, but we had to ask legends themselves what was it about their nickname that stuck and made them powerful to the folks they interacted with.

Were they self proclaimed? Or given? Were they more from when they were younger or were they given to them in college? Names and nicknames are powerful because not only do they endear people to you, they're also a strong relationship builder and networking tool that can lead you to job opportunities after college.

In 2012, I was hosting the Midwest Entrepreneurs Conference in Omaha, NE. It was a conference full of undergraduate students and entrepreneurs presenting about businesses they had started. That morning, to get the event off to a quick start, I did an energizer for folks sitting next to each other. I had them share a nickname they have or had in their life and the significance or history of that nickname. Later in that day, one of the speakers, Frank, was discussing a business relationship he developed with a potential customer. They went out on the town.

As the story goes, when Frank called the guy several months later, he got the secretary and was put on hold. When the secretary came back, she said the guy was busy and couldn't take his call. But Frank was persistent.

He said to her, "Tell him it's Frank The Tank from Vegas." As soon as she went back and told the guy, he picked up the line and began yelling on the phone, "Frank the Tank, how the hell are you?" As soon as he told that part of the story I jumped up out of my seat and everyone began laughing because we clearly saw the purpose of the morning activity as it pertains to building a brand, a business, and Legendary Status on campus.

Even though for me, names and nicknames have always had high importance, when an entrepreneur is able to get a foot in the door, be memorable, make a sale and maintain a new relationship all because of a nickname, I think the group really understands how powerful nicknames are.

As we mentioned in Chapter 1, names are powerful so we must try hard to value people's namesakes and remember **who they are**. The beautiful thing about it is that now we have social media platforms that never really allow you to forget, so our networks are bigger and better than ever.

If you want to become Legendary, make sure you're taking advantage of all these outlets to build your personal brand. A lot of Facebook famous people are now including their nickname as part of their profile, which continually pushes the message you're trying to convey to others.

Perception does become reality in the social media world and that's why it's so powerful now.

2.4 Is your brand sustainable?

Your name and face are clearly important and memorable! But the establishment of a **true** personal brand in the realm of your academic experience can be crucial to becoming LEGENDARY! So our question for you is: if someone is talking about *you*, will they know it's you based on something you always do, always say, your nickname, or an object that's linked to you?

Can you be nameless and still be identified on campus? This whole concept of building a brand during high school and college is a complete game changer as I look back at what took place in college at UNO. The brand I was able to build and the networks I established benefited me well *after* college. This is the goal!

How do you set yourself up through great personal branding and established relationships so that after college your network remains tight and your opportunities to get a job remain high?

It's important to consider building a brand by choosing *where* you go to college. The most basic example I can give is comparing the University of Nebraska Lincoln and the University of Nebraska Omaha. It's the ultimate comparison of a University in a "college town" vs. a "metropolitan university."

Oftentimes this is the decision between a "traditional" college experience and maybe an alternative one. I personally felt (as a business student at UNO) that I had an advantage over business students at Nebraska Lincoln and here's why:

I had an internship through INROADS for 4 years of college in Omaha. I worked for Cox Communications and Kutak Rock in Omaha throughout those years. During those four years I had the opportunity to work 20 hours a week during the school year and 40 hours during the summer. Most business students who were interning from UNL were not doing it in Lincoln. Let's be real; most of the jobs and opportunities in Nebraska exist in Omaha. So students who chose UNL for school would come back to intern in Omaha during the summer. Once their summer was over they'd go back to school working their on-campus job or working at the bar.

Me? I continued building valuable relationships, proving myself, having lunch with my supervisors, networking with other HR representatives who recruited professionals in Omaha, getting benefits like tuition reimbursement and making $9/hour in 2002 (which was good money at that time).

I was able to start and complete projects at my internships and I never had to pass off a project due to having to go back to school. I felt all these things were crucial to me preparing for success after graduation.

I hope you can see the potential value in considering personal brand and relationship building in college *as a choice*. This is the new choice. Where can you set yourself up to have the most personal success, keep your debt low, build a personal brand, and graduate?

I think building a personal brand like this is putting your support behind the people you're going to school with. Building a network on campus with young leaders who will be taking over the world is visionary!

Every move I make through Passion for Leadership and through The Future Project as a Dream Director is for the next generation of hungry, passionate students who will be running the world in 15 years when I need them and they'll say that, 'Lamarr had my back when I was 15 and it meant a lot to me, so I have his back now!'

These are not often decisions made by parents and students. Jono and I were able to create brand recognition at UNO partly because we were big fish in a small sea. At UNO, there were 12,500 students. Not the smallest sea but smaller than UNL. I personally think I could have re-created what we built at UNO on any campus. You have to consider colleges and universities the size of Nebraska Lincoln (25,000) or even the University of Wisconsin (50,000). Is it possible to create a personal brand at institutions bigger than most towns in the state? Absolutely.

And it all adds to your LEGENDARY STATUS!

Legendary Lesson 3 – How to Discover Your LEADERSHIP Story

3.1 How we discovered our leadership styles

During interviews with former and current student legends from all over the country, almost all of them went to college right after high school with the intention of being **the** man, the woman, or the person! Most of them literally said, "I want to run this campus!"

What an audacious, confident and rather presumptuous statement to make as an 18-year-old college freshman. This led us to believe that if you want to be LEGENDARY, you have to want it at some level.

The path you choose to become legendary is completely up to you. When you know what you want, you don't waste time and energy on things you don't care about.

Although Jono and I ended up as orientation leaders and shared similarities with regard to our People Philosophy, we ended up as legends through a slightly different mindset. So, we're going to share two separate philosophies on pursuing leadership on campus or at work that will allow you to identify which side you actually fall on.

Lamarr

During my high school years I would not have called myself a "leader" by any means. I played basketball in 9th and 10th grade and then quit my junior year during tryouts because I thought I was going to get cut.

"Can't cut me, I quit."

Lol. *Right*. Immediately after I quit, I joined DECA, which is a club for students interested in marketing and business.

I was also slightly involved with the student council my sophomore and junior years. I always participated, but I never led. I don't know if I was scared to lead (or at least be labeled the leader) but honestly, it was never something I wanted to take on. I never wanted additional responsibility.

Weird, right? How can you be a legendary leader and not lead anyone or be the President or Vice President of a student organization? I never really thought about it until I got to college and "leadership" seemed to become a buzz word more than it ever had in high school.

In the process of writing this book and continuing to analyze my own experience to evolve my speaking message, I started to recognize the qualities about myself that helped me become LEGENDARY! In high school, I never led anybody but I bridged gaps between groups of people. I created community, family amongst strangers, comfortable environments for all to be themselves freely. I am now seeing this was my biggest leadership quality.

As I stepped onto the college scene, I forged a goal that would require me to once again create communities. I wanted to meet as many people as I could who did not go to my high school. Remember that? I mentioned that earlier. Yes, that was my goal and there were a couple of issues with that happening at a fast rate.

First, I was commuting from home and not living on campus my freshman year. Second, UNO at the time was just transitioning to a campus that provided residence halls so the perception was that student life wasn't the greatest. Orientation was a great way for me to trump not living on campus because I had a chance to meet droves of incoming freshmen. We were always the craziest, most risqué/outrageous in our comments and the most memorable of our entire orientation crew. Of course, I have to give props to Tom Centarri, Adam Hamilton, and Dave Jarvis as well. These gentlemen were heavyweights in the game.

Going into my second year as an orientation leader, I was introduced to the student organization side of being an orientation leader. It was time to run for an officer position within SOLO, but I ran away from leadership responsibilities again.

I didn't mind more responsibility; I just didn't want to be responsible for formalized leadership. I didn't want to go to meetings; I knew I wouldn't go anyway. I didn't want to have to plan fundraising events. I didn't want to have meetings with the orientation advisor. All I wanted to do was get in front of people and welcome them to our campus in a way that made them feel like this was about the best four years of their life. That's what I loved, that's what I wanted to do!

So, instead of taking on a leadership position, I went and found another way to be in front of people. I went and became a UNO Matador! Matadors were the students who gave tours to prospective high school students, transfer students, and their parents. Giving tours allowed me to get better at my craft as an orientation leader. It also gave me the opportunity to be in front of the same audience before they even got to New Student Orientation.

It was my job to sell the experience. Think about the sequence of events here. My goal was to meet as many people as possible. I became an orientation leader, which allowed me to meet almost every freshman or transfer student who came to UNO. I then began giving tours to the very students who would ultimately end up attending new student orientation and finally choose the University of Nebraska Omaha.

People loved my charisma, my knowledge of the campus, and my ability to relate to them no matter where they came from. I always said that if UNO would have paid me commissions for every student who chose UNO after a tour with me, I would have been a rich man in college.

It was after my second year as an orientation leader and my first as a Matador that I realized I didn't want to lead by being the stereotypical leader. I wanted to put all my energy into the jobs I loved most. I wanted to lead by being the absolute best of the best.

I didn't want to lead by being the President of SOLO, but I wanted to be the best orientation leader who had ever walked the halls of UNO's campus. This was the choice I was making on how I wanted to lead, knowing myself and learning what I wanted to do and what I wanted to do made it very easy to concentrate on being the best and simply leading by example.

During my third year of college, I became a Resident Assistant (RA). Mainly, I did it for free rent but this position allowed me to have a third and final touch point with incoming students, which cemented my relationship with them and their parents (at that point). The trust was there and the relationships were very easy to maintain after that.

The biggest advantage to this was that, outside of the students they met at their orientation, the only person they knew when they got back to campus in the fall was their orientation leader. At this point, they knew who we were and it mattered if we remembered their names and who they were. Often, we did. Jono and I thrived in this environment

Being self aware allows you to know *exactly* what you want and make confident decisions about your future.

Jono

When Lamarr and I sat down to talk about our experiences, we really wanted to show young leaders a holistic view of how leaders can show up. Different situations require different types of leadership, so being exposed to it all is beneficial. When you think of what kind of leader you want to be, most times it's not up to you, but rather it's a calling that's just a part of you. For me, I never wanted to be just a number and I hate wasting time, so stepping up to the plate and being a leader to get things done wasn't ever an issue. I just did it. I would see a problem and be the one to lead the troops to get it resolved. I was also called upon by my peers and professors/administrators to be the one to lead the charge. So, like I stated before, sometimes it really isn't up to you, it's just what needs to be done.

When I look back as to what kind of leader I was in college, it simply came down to me caring for every single person I met no matter who they were and also in wanting to take charge. But it's deeper than just putting my style of leadership into one category.

I'll explain.

I believe that most students go to college with a vision of what they want to accomplish in their years on campus and, for most, I'd imagine it's a dream of earning a degree and going onto a successful career after they've had a little fun. My outlook was somewhat different because every time I was asked what I wanted to do, I would always reply with the same answer: "I want to make a difference in the world."

The reason I point that out is because (for me), I knew the minute I stepped onto my college campus I needed to start practicing what I was preaching. But also, it wasn't like an equation I had to figure out; it just came naturally by simply caring for each person who I came in contact with.

In fact, the first person I ever spoke to at my university was one of the ladies who worked at the registrar's office and I never forgot how welcoming she was so I would make sure to drop in from time to time and bring her muffins and coffee. Now, I did this not to get favors (to be honest), but because if I was nice to her, she would be a good connection for me and what I would be trying to accomplish throughout my upcoming college years. This is who I was, a person that no matter who you were, I wanted to know you and figure out a way to better support you.

Okay, so now I'm on campus and everything is going smoothly through my first few weeks. I had some interesting classes, met some cool people, but I wasn't making an impact ... yet.

Then it hit me: *find solutions to people's issues.*

If I knew a math major who was broke and I knew a student who was struggling in math, then why not connect them? One got some extra cash for tutoring and the other had the chance to earn a passing grade.

Or I would help facilitate two students who needed to find a way to get into a certain dorm because it was closer to the majority of the buildings they had classes in. All I would do is ensure that I got the student in front of the housing director (who I happened to know) all by simply talking to them. Just like that, a student's life was a little better.

It didn't even have to be anything like that; it could have been finding out a student's dream of being at the halftime show during a big game. Knowing the production crew needed a shocking reaction caught on camera, I would ensure that their ticket was "randomly" picked.

How would I pull things off like that? Once again, it was simply just caring and listening to what each party needed (or wanted). I would do things like this all the time and it was just that I never stopped caring about making a difference.

People would ask me all the time why I did things like this because I never got anything out of it. But that's where they couldn't be more wrong. I got more out of it than the people who I connected to others. I was able to know that I helped people get through a difficult time or helped someone in some way. So, through the course of all of this, I hope I was able to help enough students, that when they left college, they were able to make a difference in the world. Full-circle of giving.

3.2 What is your best leadership style?

The opposite of self-centered leadership (which, honestly, is not necessarily a form of leadership but one we made up) is **others-centered leadership**. In our view, you can tell when someone is in an organization for the love and passion of creating something awesome and being part of a team or when they're self-absorbed, want all the credit, and aren't sure how to empower others to be great. Granted, college students are young and developing.

That's the point of this book: **to teach students how to live their life to the fullest, love and lead people in a way that is inspiring, fulfilling and gets stuff done.** When I talk to students about leadership, we specifically talk about six leadership styles that we analyze with our students:

1) Affiliative Leader
2) Authoritative Leader
3) Pacesetting Leader
4) Coaching Leader
5) Coercive Leader
6) Democratic Leader

We know effective leadership can show up in many ways. Realistically, every organization is different and has a different group of individuals that make up the organization. Arguably, it seems nearly impossible to make everyone happy but part of what we know is that good leadership is execution and empathy and it really takes a set of special leadership skills to be able to implement your own leadership style.

I have a strong opinion about how each type of leader is laid out in front of you and I'll break down each one.

Affiliative Leaders, in my eyes, always start off as the best-supporting type of leader we all need, but later can become the star. A lot of times there's a vision of what needs to be done, but no one knows how to accomplish it. That's when an Affiliative Leader steps up. Usually, these types of leaders are very organized, intelligent, good listeners and can get the "buy in" from others.

A good example of this type of leadership is Thomas Jefferson. Now, I don't think anyone would consider him a supporting role, but at first he was counted on to shape the message and vision that the group was thinking, but didn't know how to make it work. This allowed him to step up and become even stronger as a leader because they understood the situation better than anyone in the room. I honestly believe without Affiliative Leaders, a lot of great ideas would not get accomplished.

I feel that we have all known an **Authoritative Leader** in our lifetime. This is a person who is usually smart, charismatic enough to get people to believe in them, and is quick enough to think on his/her feet. In my eyes, this is the one type of leader who is misunderstood by several people. At times, they get a rap as being a class-clown or a distraction, but if they lead the mood correctly, they can accomplish a lot of good just by being themselves. While taking charge, they have to be confident in who they are and what they stand for, knowing that they're putting themselves on a ledge. In this type of leadership, there truly is not an in-between with them as to what they have passion for. Either they are a class-clown or they are a visionary who understands the issue and is a voice for the people.

I believe that **Pacesetting Leaders** are good candidates to become future employees of the State Department or CEOs of companies. I believe this because they are the type of leaders who do their homework *before* they speak up and can debate the issue. No one ever will question their intelligence or their knowledge on a subject when they chime in. Pacesetting Leaders are well-read on several different subjects and may be one of the best people to have a five-minute conversation with at a cocktail party. The one flaw they may have is the fact that (at times), they go ahead with an idea prior to getting the "buy-in" from others or gather enough support to take on a major situation.

The last type of leader is referred to as a **Coaching Leader**, which in my eyes may be the most well-rounded leader we've discussed. These are the types of people who can walk into a room and simply own it by just being who they are. They don't have to try to be anyone other than themselves because they're that confident in who they are, what they bring to the table and, most importantly, they know how to relate to just about anyone. Coaching Leaders are also people who can make a stranger feel calm and at ease about a big problem they're facing by simply showing that they're not in it alone. Coaching Leaders are also known for being "big idea" people and usually want to see everyone around them succeed in whatever direction they want to go.

These are the types of leaders that immediately gain trust with people around them and can make sure they feel confident while talking through any situation. It's because of this that these types of leaders have a 'we win as a team' attitude to accomplish their goals. A person that comes to mind is one of the best coaches of all times, the legendary Tennessee Lady Vols basketball coach, Pat Summitt.

When the Sporting News put together the 50 greatest coaches of all time, she was on it, and I must add, that she was the only woman on the list. When she retired due to her Alzheimer's diagnosis, she had three national titles under her belt and was beloved by her university, basketball fans all over the world and mostly anyone who had the opportunity to hear her speak. She did such great things that in 2012 she was awarded the Presidential Medal of Freedom by Barack Obama. When she passed away, many people spoke about her basketball successes, but more talked about how she simply cared for everyone she had a connection with. And as a coach, I believe she would have been more proud of how many souls she touched compared to how many victories she took home for the Volunteers.

A good example of a **Coaching Leader**, it's how she was able to get the "buy-in" from any of her players, coaching staff and the school. If you're looking to be a good leader while having tremendous success, try to talk and understand what everyone's saying to you while getting them to believe in you, just like the great, late Pat Summitt did for so many years.

The **Coercive Leader** (in my eyes) is more of a manager and not as much of a natural leader. To me, this is someone who leads out of fear, much like a manager does with little feedback on what everyone thinks should happen. When I think of a Coercive Leader, I think of a person who threatens his/her team in order to get things done and sees a lot of success at getting projects completed or accomplished in a timely manner, but not necessarily out or respect from both sides.

A **Democratic Leader**, to me, is the one who is "next in line" to take charge. I feel these types of leaders step up because they're in the right place at the right time when something needs to be done or when a captain is needed. To me, this is someone who doesn't have a passion for the end goal enough to put themselves out there prior to getting asked to, but can get to the finish line because they understand what needs to be done.

There is no one leadership style that can capture your style, personality or experiences for which you lead but we wanted to give you a foundation to start evaluating the type of leader you are. This can then morph into the kind of leader you want to become in the future.

3.3 How to step up your CREATIVITY game!

I've done keynotes speeches and workshops on campuses around the country over the last five years and, typically, it's the same old tune when it comes to college leadership. The same passionate leaders are the most engaged and are also doing most of the work and showing up to most of the meetings. Student organizations are lacking money, time, members, processes and structure. The most important thing I've noticed in my work with college students is a serious lack of creativity in trying to solve these challenges within their organizations.

If you want to be a legendary leader on campus, at the very least, be an executor. If you can be an executor and also an innovator and create new ways to solve traditional problems that all organizations face, you'll be **legendary**.

You have to be someone who thinks outside the box at all times (or at least surround yourself with people who are consistently innovative and not afraid to try new things). Basically, if you want to change the game, you have to do cool stuff. You'll know when it's cool because everyone will want to do it and be part of it. We mentioned it earlier that movements start on college campuses.

If you want to start a revolution, a college campus is the place to do it no matter what you want to do. Many times, when you're trying to do cool stuff. you have to be first in the game to capitalize on what's happening, especially to your world, industry or organizational focus.

If you're at the heart of the conversation and paying attention to what's happening in your space, your passion will lead you to doing creative things by nature; you'll know how to innovate within that conversation.

Keys to Creative Thinking

1) STOP KILLING IDEAS BECAUSE YOU DON'T THINK IT'S A GOOD ONE. Most student organizations are typically full of opinions and, at times, differing opinions. Knowing this, you're bound to have pessimistic idea killers. You want to stop creativity? Shut down ideas *before* you've had any chance to talk about them in greater detail and make assumptions about what's needed to make that idea a reality. INSTEAD, flesh ideas out, discuss every idea and when you do that it may turn into something you never thought it would or could and that might just be perfect.

2) ARE YOU DOING THE OBVIOUS or WHAT HAS WORKED FOR OTHERS? I was speaking at a leadership day at a Midwest university and during the workshop involving creativity, a group of leaders were seriously concerned about trying to raise money for their organization. I asked them a series of questions about what they were raising money for and how much they actually needed, which was about $300, which, in my opinion, is not a lot of money. So I asked, "Have you started crowdfunding from websites like go.fund.me or kickstarter.com?" They said no. I realized that not

everyone is aware of all the resources out there, so it's important to know when it's all said and done you explored quite a few opportunities. GOOGLE IT! Also, what are you willing to do to get the money? Will you ask random strangers on campus to donate and support your efforts? What about in the local community? Will you ask your family? How many businesses will you solicit?

3) BE ORIGINAL. Revolutions start on campus by not being scared to push the envelope or push a couple buttons in the face of creativity; this is a great way to move past fear. As they say, if it doesn't scare you then the idea isn't big enough. One of the most epic revolutions we have seen on a college campus (in my opinion) is the four basketball guys known as the "Monmouth Bench." Google them. In 2016, these guys took the country by storm with their creativity and are inspiring everyone they know to support people and not be afraid to push the envelope. Every time their teams scored or made a great defensive play, 3-5 guys at the end of the bench that never played created different group celebrations they would do in the middle of games. Don't you think these guys had second thoughts about acting too goofy on the bench or not taking the game seriously enough for their coach, especially if one of them had a chance to play? There's a bigger picture here. Don't more guys see how cool or fun it is to play at Monmouth? Don't you think that their coach allowing them to do this

was raising his own profile as well as that of the university? Revolutions like this can happen at any moment and all it takes is collective creativity and courage to go against the grain or the status quo!

3.4 The Future of Leadership and Work

In my experience in college at the University of Nebraska at Omaha, I feel like there were leaders on campus who didn't quite understand what leadership was. Part of college is gaining the experiences that it takes to be a strong leader and not only a strong leader but to be Legendary Leaders. In today's share and gig economy and also with the type of workforce students will be graduating into, we're seeing less reliance on individual leaders and are moving toward a model of lateral leadership and collaboration that doesn't require as much top-down leadership. What this means is that if you're looking to model leadership, you really need to be a leader who **coaches and empowers** and not demands and is never seen.

We're seeing the share economy allow for more autonomy and also young visionaries leading organizations but also being part of the fabric as regular employees. Knowing that this is where we're headed in the future with a more modern workforce and way of working, it's important for you to know the value of different types of leadership during college.

As generation Z'ers, we're expecting a lot more out of your leadership. We're demanding partnership instead of traditional leadership. We want to feel like we're helping to create something with upper-level leadership. We want to work in offices side-by-side with our CEOs. We want to be able to email our VPs directly and have a personal relationship with them. We want people to do business with and feel like there's a more human connection there.

We want to explore our passions at work which allow us to want to be at work more and do the work we're required to do harder for our employers. The new kind of leadership in the coming era does not provide for Authoritative or Coercive leaders anymore. That style is slowly dying amongst the power companies in America today. The Googles, the Facebooks, the Vaynermedias of the world. We're looking for leaders that execute on a high level but also care to coach and develop and lend major responsibility to the young talent that companies are hiring.

Entrepreneur Gary Vaynerchuck writes about social media and business. Specifically, he often refers to social media as a wine party where you get to flirt with everyone and get to know something about everybody. As leaders, you have the ability to do this in person and on social media to build your personal brand but also strengthen your leadership qualities. Legends should always be seeking common ground with people that you don't know.

There's no easier way to get down to business than to talk about everything *except* business. People may think I'm pretty intense but when I'm in social settings, especially now, I try to avoid asking the most common question young professionals ask, "So, what do you do?" I encourage you to ask any other open-ended question about their life. It forces them to be real with you and perhaps allows them to not have a conversation they have all the time.

Take a course on coaching, develop yourself so you see your own blindspots, and don't be scared to be wrong. Surround yourself with people who fill gaps outside your own strengths. Lend responsibility to others and let them fail and coach them. Developing leaders starts by recognizing when someone needs *you* to step up and impact their life.

Legendary Lesson 4 - How to Make Everyone Feel INCLUDED!

4.1 How to build community with inclusive language

Inclusive language is critical to creating a positive culture on campus and in organizations. Visionary leaders are constantly speaking about how the team operates together and impacts each member. If you want people to believe in you, your language is key.

I see it so many times when I'm talking to student organizations -on campuses, particularly- leadership is engaged in language that excludes the group and separates them from members. It's more than valuable that your language be consistent and that you use words like 'we,' 'us,' 'the group,' 'the team,' 'the family,' 'the squad,' 'the crew,' 'together,' etc.

Avoid words like I, me, you, exec team, etc. at all cost because it will separate you from them, members from leadership, the team from the department. Naturally, some of this will happen from time to time (and be necessary), but your language can and will set the tone for how you operate.

One of the greatest stories of inclusivity I've seen on a campus came from my friends down at Fort Hays State BSU. I'll never forget this story. The President of the FHSU Black Student Union in 2011 was Vernon Johnson and when I was speaking at FHSU that year he was telling a story from the beginning of the school year while the group was recruiting new members, which I believe set the tone for BSU and the identity of the group.

He mentioned how a young lady, she was white, approached him and asked, "Don't you have to be black to be part of the Black Student Union?" He said, 'Well yeah if you are BLACK, I mean BOLD, LIVELY, ALLURING, CREATIVE and KIND then yeah, you do have to be black!' At that moment the young lady signed up to be a part of BSU at Fort Hays. Two years later she became the president of the FHSU BSU. Talk about inclusivity, talk about togetherness, talk about language that inspires and creates a culture of welcoming within your student's organization.

This is simply one of the greatest tone setters for any student organization that I have ever heard in all of my time working on campuses! The idea of taking an age-old problem that most BSUs probably face on campuses all over America and using the word BLACK to empower not just young black college students but also *all* those interested in the culture, life, and history of African Americans on campus.

Currently, college campuses are growing while having to also learn how to accommodate and create inclusive communities. Your leadership style and ability

must match up with what is currently happening on campus from a social perspective.

We're talking about academic inequality amongst minority students, first generation students, and LGBTQIA+ students on campuses, supportive learning communities, and the rising costs of education that are all topics hitting campuses hard and that need the new form of leadership Gen Z'ers can provide, but it begins with you recognizing everyone for who they are and them recognizing you for who you are.

Over the last five years, I've seen racial tensions in our society get worse but when I step on campuses around the country I see pockets of solidarity and people coming together to fight for what's right. Did I say that revolutions start on college campuses? Take a look, for example, at the young man Jonathan Butler from Omaha who went to Mizzou and went on a hunger strike until the chancellor of the university stepped down for poorly handling terrible racial crimes committed on campus. It's up to college students and incoming leaders to be LEGENDARY and start a movement when the opportunity arises, especially when you're passionate about what you're fighting for or what you love.

I do believe that inclusivity = love and love and acceptance can solve a lot of problems. It's up to the current generation of youth to get our country through this hard time and although there are many areas to work on, we must recognize the past and acknowledge where we are currently as a result of that past, but we must also continue to be forward-thinking about how we can create inclusivity and creative solutions to problems involving religion, race, sexuality, identity, and any other social issues that require our attention in the next five years!

Are you ready to be a LEGENDARY leader? The challenges of your time on campus are unmatched to when Jono and I were in college. Now is your time to take control and blaze your own trail in the world.

4.2 How to build community through shared rituals

One thing I've learned over the last few years while developing young leaders is that you can create inclusivity deliberately. This is all part of building a culture.

One way to forge culture is to create norms or rituals within your organizations. Fraternities, sororities, ROTC organizations and sports teams are very good at accomplishing this, which all bring people together. Fraternities and sororities often have roll calls, wear their letters, or create certain handshakes and nicknames that are only used by people within that organization.

Sports teams use chants or dances to get them excited and hyped up for a game or practice. It's all about motivation, like the first steps into a new world when it's game time.

In so many instances, organizations in high schools and colleges lack the passion and commitment that our sports teams and Greek organizations have. The question is, *how do you create that passion, energy and excitement with organizations that create the inclusivity you're looking for that welcomes everyone and helps them feel connected to your organization?*

If you've ever played a sport or were part of a Greek organization, this could be a great way to establish togetherness, create community, create a safe space, create a sacred space and actually create an expectation or something to look forward to; it allows you to (literally) create a norm that could lead to autonomy amongst your organization. Also, it gives your group pride, particularly amongst groups that are similar.

Keys to building rituals:

1) One moment of collective touch.

When I say 'one moment of collective touch,' everyone must touch at some point during the ritual. Often, this can look like holding hands, linking arms at the elbows, or everyone in the group creating a huddle, or all hands in the center of a circle. Make sure your 'moment of touch' is not confused with your moment of movement (although you will probably move when you do touch); just keep in mind that it's separate. Also keep in mind everyone's right to choose not to participate in any physical touch activity as well.

2) One moment of collective voice.

When I say 'one moment of collective voice,' this refers to the group's chance to amplify your message or your catchphrase. Create your chant! Have fun with this.

This -combined with collective movement- is what really gets the situation into full hype! For example, every Monday, Dream Directors in NYC start and end our meeting with a ritual that sets the tone for our team identity and our meeting that day. Our collective voice sounds like this, "We Epic, We, We Epic – Be Epic, Be, Be Epic, Dream Epic, Dream, Dream Epic – E – P – I – C!" The moment of collective voice should speak directly to the theme of the year for your team. It should remind everyone of the mission or why you do it. It should get you excited and pumped to do the work that's required of you in that moment.

3) One moment of collective movement.

Lean side to side, do the running man, do the wave. Just move! One of my fellow motivational speakers, Laymon Hicks, does a great job of this at the beginning of all his speeches and it sets the tone for the rest of the time students will spend together. He asks students to lock arms at the shoulders and start swaying from one side to the other. He then hits the button to the song "Swag Surfin" and they're off with the collective energy at 1,000%! Movement is essential to the ritual and when you put it all together it allows you to create your own excitement for the work that needs to be done.

4.3 Integrity - Your WORD is Your BOND!

Are you an executor? At any level, are you someone who does what they say they will do? Are you someone who makes big promises or goals and typically follows through on them? Execute within your word and your leadership will speak for itself.

In the summer of 2017, I took a personal development course called the Landmark Forum. It taught me a lot about integrity. In my keynotes around leadership, I often talk about the definition of integrity. I always ask students what it means to them. The answer I get most often is, "Doing the right thing when nobody's watching," or, "Doing what you say you're going to do," which are both good definitions.

The word integrity comes from the word INTEGER and integer means "to be whole," or another way of looking at it is to "be complete."

I often describe it as being consistent in leadership and treating everyone as equals, not being too hot or too cold or always back and forth in your personality. But after I took this course, I realized that my old definition wasn't off track but there was a whole new meaning. At 32 years of age, I learned the importance of your word and the value people place on it when you say you will do something, especially when you're leading or when someone trusts you or someone really loves you. Not keeping your word can be a serious letdown for some folks. The reason I was never let down by others' word was because I never really valued my own word.

As I sat in the Landmark Forum on the last day of the seminar, two major clues hit me square in the face and it changed the way I viewed integrity. My friends sent a message in group chat about everybody meeting up and since I live in a different city, they knew I was not going to be there, but they also followed it up with a meme that said, *"When you got that friend that's always late!"* And it hit me, my blindspot in leadership that I completely had been missing for years: I was too busy yolo'ing and not thinking about being late or appearing not to respect people's time or thinking it was no big deal that my friends began to de-value my word.

And when I would show up late to my team meetings because I was coming from the farthest distance, there was a possibility that my word was starting to mean nothing to them as well. So, what I learned about leading and leadership at 32 that I am lending to you right now is that **you *must* first value your word to yourself before it can be of value to others**.

I consistently broke my word (to myself), which created a habit of breaking my word or agreement with others and I never realized it until people just flat out said *I don't believe you*. This was one of the most profound things I had to learn about leadership and life. Sallome Hralima, National Dream Director for The Future Project always says to Dream Directors, "Where is your word if it's not in your mouth?"

Let me give you a basic example (not in leadership, per se) that can help you practice keeping your word in life, which will allow you to help keep it in leadership. I had to learn this from my partner because it was another example of me breaking my word and not fixing it.

Often, when I travel back to Nebraska from NYC, I attend fish fries, which Jono first invited me to many, many years ago. I ran into a young man at the fish fry the last time I was in Nebraska. His name was Charlie; he was about 15. He and a friend were off looking at a text message while they were helping clean up the fish fry and I overheard him say, "Geez, is it not okay that I'm volunteering? I can't believe she's mad about this!"

As they walked closer to us, I had to grab the young boy and school him on how this could work out better for him in the future. I said, 'Charlie, why is your girlfriend mad at you?' He said, 'She's mad because we were supposed to watch a movie and I wasn't supposed to be here this late.' I asked, 'Did you commit to the movie before you knew you had to volunteer at the fish fry?' He said he did. I said to him, 'So here's your challenge. You committed to watching a movie when you really weren't sure what time you would be getting done volunteering. Now you're out of integrity with someone who cares about you and that person is not mad that you're volunteering but because you committed to something and can't follow through on it.' I told him he would have been better off not committing to the movie that night because he had no idea how long he would be volunteering. At this point he said, 'Yeah, that makes a lot of sense.'

And I said, "Man, that advice right there will literally change your life!"

In leadership, if you want to be a LEGENDARY leader, keep your word! **Underpromise and overdeliver!** At all costs *do not do it the other way around.* The value of your word is linked to the respect people have for you and any organization that you're affiliated with. If your word is your bond, your word is gold in the eyes of those who follow you because they trust beyond a shadow of a doubt that you will follow through on what you say you're going to do. When you execute on your word and you care about people creating that social capital, they will follow you anywhere you're trying to lead them. You'll make them feel included by showing them you keep your word (to them).

PASSION leads to ACTION which leads to MOMENTUM which leads to CONFIDENCE

As leaders, oftentimes we're expected to always be 'on' and most of the time we are! Especially if you're trying to become a LEGEND on campus. Trying to manage social, academics, and leadership responsibilities while dealing with personal things at home or in your life can be extremely challenging. There will be moments when you are **off**.

You have to know that this is *okay.* Leading humans and finding what you love and being creative and balancing all of it is **hard** but this is how leaders become LEGENDS (when you bounce back from failure or from adversity stronger than you went in).

There will be peaks and valleys, there will be ups and downs, there will be successes and failures, there will be ideas that work and ideas that won't work. Here's what I can share with you because you can know this for sure: when you want something bad enough, when you love something enough, when you have passion keeping you up at night working on a project, you will continue to act and move toward your goals. This way when you're in action toward your goals there is no time to think about the past and any past failures and struggles.

Creating new possibilities allows you to always move forward and not be a victim to what happened yesterday like so many of us are. When you're in action, it gives you momentum and when you have momentum, you have confidence and when you have confidence, you feel like anything and everything you touch can and will turn to gold. You will walk boldly in the direction of your dreams when you do this.

And when those moments come and you aren't in the "flow" or, as Shonda Rhimes called it, "the hum," you'll realize it's okay because you're playing the long game. You're running a marathon, 26.2 miles, you're in it for the long haul and when you commit, not one thing can shake your confidence because you know and believe that if you're down and out now you have what it takes to stay the course!

4.4. How to run your meeting like a boss

Learning how to run a meeting properly is a skill you'll need if you're going to become a Legendary Leader! Many student organizations follow Roberts' rules of order, especially our student governments and fraternal organizations. To me, those old traditional ways are played out. You need to educate, entertain, and inspire in all your meetings, if possible.

Here's a framework for meetings that could work for your team:

1. **Icebreaker** - always start with some fun, energized or reflection activity.
2. **Updates/Announcements** - inform the group of important happenings that could be impactful or beneficial to people in the group.
3. **Activity** - the intentional learning or action-based activities that you want to do during your meeting.
4. **Shoutouts** - show you teammates and constituents love.
5. **Ritual** - always end or begin your meeting with some ritual that signifies your collective group or team.

Here are a few different types of meeting structures you might find yourself leading as a Legendary Leader:

There are three main types of experiences you will have to lead.

Meetings
Good for planning and getting work done. Examples of this are DT meetings, teacher meetings, event committee meetings, etc.

Workshops
Good for learning and practicing new skills or ideas. Ex. training, or classes.

Circles
Good for reflection on what has happened and how to make it better.

A few tips on building leadership capital on campus.

- Always give credit and recognition to your team; when they win you are also winning.
- Always ask everyone you meet on campus if there's anything you can do for them.
- Before you complain about something going on within your organization, always have an alternative solution prepared to positively contribute to solving the problem.

Legendary Lesson 5 – How and Why Empathy Matters in Leadership to Execute!

5.1 Three Empathy Skills That Matter

- Icebreakers
- Coaching/Goal Map
- Managing Disagreements, Conflicts and Negotiations

In 2008, when I started speaking around the country I was giving student leadership advice based on my own experience in high school and college. In 2013, I moved to New York City to work for a start-up education non-profit called the Future Project to be a Dream Director in a New York City high school in Washington Heights.

At the beginning, our mandate from the CEO was that Dream Directors disrupt the monotony of school and inspire students and staff to dream their biggest dreams and discover their deepest passions and then coach them toward making them a reality.

I really concentrated during my first couple of years around helping kids pursue their dreams, but what I found was that my ability to coach didn't always fit so nicely within a school schedule.

Since it was my full-time job to help students pursue their dreams, I typically found myself doing most of the work toward that dream (whatever it was), which was not doing the students justice.

During my third year, I started leaning toward training students on mindsets and skill sets that could provide them a framework they could remember easily and utilize for the rest of their life to actually make their dreams happen. This felt more valuable. Specifically, I had a **framework** for students to write proposals for projects they wanted to create so they could formally send them to the principal. At the same time, I had a few committees of student leaders working on school-wide initiatives. One of those students leading a committee on bringing in inspirational speakers to talk to the school was one of my top sophomores, Javier Molina. Javier's first order of business was to bring in a speaker starting in December of 2015.

I checked in with Javier multiple times between December and February and he still hadn't reached out to the speaker we agreed on. I finally sat him down for a real coaching conversation and asked what was holding him back. He responded hesitantly by telling me he actually didn't know how to write an email to contact someone he didn't know and that he didn't want to sound dumb by not telling me in the first place. I was truly blown away after he told me that. At that moment, it fundamentally changed the way I was doing my job as a Dream Director. Three things happened in this scenario that gave me my 'aha' moment:

1) I made assumptions about what he knew how to do. Never assume, just ask where their comfort level is.
2) If you're going to help students pursue their dreams, they actually need to know how to write emails to people they don't know; they need to know how to get things rolling. That means they need to be **trained**.
3) Most students don't know how to advocate for themselves and their wants or needs. Let me rephrase: *most of us don't know how to advocate for ourselves.* Self advocacy is a mindset that helps you believe that you're worthy and that you deserve to learn new things and can figure out where to get answers if you don't know. This has to be taught and it takes three to four years (in my experience) to convince a student in coaching and in practice for them to have a full breakthrough in self advocacy. The ones who naturally have that voice are lucky. The rest of us have to hope someone can help us find it (our voice)!

These three items are the difference between talking about leadership based on your experience and actually having to develop student leaders. You wouldn't know this unless you were on the ground every day. It fundamentally changed how I viewed student leadership forever.

So, if you want to be Legendary and, more importantly, a Leader, you must figure out what your people need to learn, help them discover their own voice and autonomous power to operate without you and give them the opportunity to get as many reps in at the gym as possible (this is figurative, so you know) so that their skills become second nature.

This is what's required if you're going to sustain a legacy and impact your school or campus. If it can happen without you then you've empowered the entire system, not just yourself or your organization!

Sustainable Skills Legendary Leaders Need to Have in Their Tool Belt

1) **Icebreakers** are much more than "breaking the ice" for a leader. Having set icebreakers in your toolbelt says a lot about you as a leader and what's needed for your team or your meeting at any moment. Having an energizer when energy is low makes leaders aware of what's happening with their people and you can pivot to what's needed. You may need to be reflective in a moment and have a reflective activity that can bring people closer together and for them to possibly share safely and openly. More vulnerability is essential to leading great teams. You should have a go-to for small groups (under 10), large groups (bigger than 10 to 50), a reflective activity, and an energizer for groups of all sizes. Check out "The Big Book of Icebreakers" for tons of options that you can choose.

2) Learning how to coach is one of the most challenging skills, but it *can* be taught and you *can* get better at it if you want to see your team develop.

First, you have to coach your team members toward a goal. It could be team goals or personal. I've found -in my experience- that coaching the whole person, not just their professional/academic life or at least what they're willing to share with you, will lead to deeper long-term relationships and trust-building. Here's a sample goal map:

GOAL MAPS & COACHING

The Goal Map for Coaching

HOW TO USE:

1. Coachee puts their name in the middle.
2. Have them spend 10 minutes adding 3-5 goals in each section.
3. Then have 3 ten second elimination rounds to have them narrow down to their top 3 goals.
4. Use the remaining goal/s as the starting point for their coaching session.

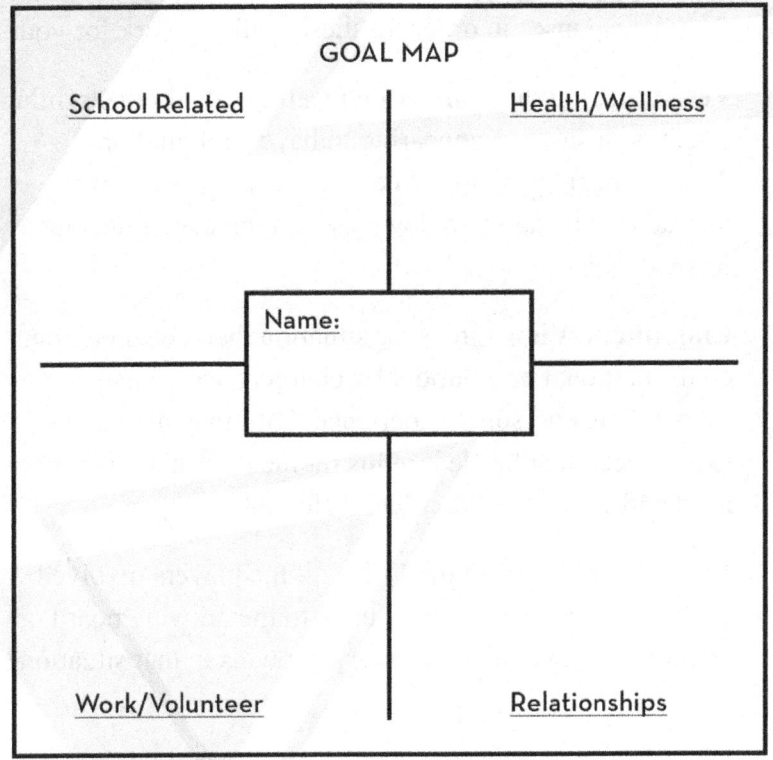

GOAL MAP

School Related

Health/Wellness

Name:

Work/Volunteer

Relationships

Once teammates have established a goal, walk them through the four-step coaching process: Inquire, Reflection, Discussion, and Make a Request.

3) Managing conflicts and disagreements is messy and for many Leaders it's not an area they want to deal with because it's hard. Particularly when you're a student leader and want to be liked by everyone, but it goes a long way toward having some negotiation skills in your pocket to push conversations forward and not come off as defensive or combative, and to be as empathetic as possible. These tips take practice and you have to build the muscle in your responses in order for these skills to work for you.

Yes and… - adding on during meetings and brainstorming sessions (instead of appearing to have a rebuttal or disagreement by saying ,"Yes, but…") opens teams up instead of closing them down by making everyone's ideas feel valuable.

Empathetic View - in every situation that's challenging, confrontational or emotionally charged, ask yourself, "What is this person's experience that I may not have experienced that has led to this moment? What might they need and want to make it feel different?"

Win-Win-Win or no deal - Do all the players involved *win*? If not, how can you go back to the drawing board or be more creative to where everyone wins in that situation?

5.2 Two Execution Skills that Matter

- Design With Intent/Crazy 8's
- Creating effective to-do lists

Creativity comes through open and free thinking, but often, as leaders, we evaluate or brainstorm in real time as opposed to letting the whole creative process happen and then evaluating fairly and not by attacking another classmate's idea or thoughts because some idea that may not be the most valuable now could be used later. So, it's essential to **let creativity reign**.

When my students and other teams are brainstorming ideas, I typically use two styles. For designing events and workshops, we use the design with intent tool. When designing for creative projects like murals (not predetermined events) I use the Crazy 8's tool. Both can help your organization collaboratively and creatively solve problems and think outside the box. More importantly, especially when dealing with young leaders, you need a democratic way of taking the best ideas and both of these strategies work to do that which leaves no one feeling like their voice wasn't heard.

Additionally, it allows everyone to contribute at their own pace. The outspoken student usually gets their idea out first versus the reserved student who may need to process and think through their thoughts *before* they make a contribution. Both of these ideas take time, but don't all great things take time? Trust the process. I'll break down further how to execute each of these tools in the **purpose and power** section.

Designing with intent is one of the most useful, practical and purposeful ways to brainstorm ideas. It's really easy. Here's a sample layout of the design with the intent tool. You could have this laid out on a whiteboard or you could do it with large self adhesive Post-Its and small Post-Its as well.

DESIGNING WITH INTENT
(WORKSHOPS/EVENTS)

INTENDED OUTCOMES

What is the purpose of this activity?

Use Post Its

IDEA #1

IDEA #2

IDEA #3

IDEA #4

IDEA #5

ACTIVITIES

How will you teach it to them?

Use Post Its

IDEA #1

IDEA #2

IDEA #3

IDEA #4

IDEA #5

OUTPUTS

What tangible artifacts will they leave with?

Use Post Its

IDEA #1

IDEA #2

IDEA #3

IDEA #4

IDEA #5

MEASURING OUTCOMES

How will you measure success?

Use Post Its

IDEA #1

IDEA #2

IDEA #3

IDEA #4

IDEA #5

IMPACT

What resulted? On your team? In your school community?

Use Post Its

IDEA #1

IDEA #2

IDEA #3

IDEA #4

IDEA #5

As a team, start to complete the DWI tool by having every student answer the questions in each category. Begin with the purpose of the activity and have everyone contribute what they believe the purpose is. Once everyone has written down their thoughts in a word or short sentence about the purpose of the event, pause there and group every Post-It note into similar themes. Let's say five themes arise. Then you vote to narrow them down to three, typically. You repeat this process all the way across the board until you've built an entire workshop, event, or week's worth of events.

The other design tool is called Crazy 8's, but you can also do Crazy 4's. This is fun because it taps into your inner artist (that you think doesn't exist, but absolutely does). Separate your members into teams or groups of three to five people per group or each person in attendance can do it individually. Groups have a design theme or question they're typically working toward. For example, this year I wanted to create a mural for our staff and teachers. We wanted the ideas to be student-led so we asked them to think of as many words as they could that conveyed how they felt about the teachers and staff at our school. They came up with a list of about 12 words to base their design brainstorm on. Once there are groups and a theme, ask each team to separate their large Post-It notes into four quadrants.

Give each team a minute to a minute-and-a-half to draw in the first square. From there, teams can either add to their first idea in the forthcoming squares or draw a completely new idea. Once all four squares are full, you ask teams to unify their best ideas to one or choose their best idea. This idea then gets voted on amongst all teams and you narrow everything down to your top one or two ideas and execute on those.

To do list and dashboards

This skill is essential to efficiency. I believe that folks have been creating personal to-do lists their whole life. Probably since you first got a planner in middle school you've had a list of things you needed to do for school, work, and life.

In 2014, as a Dream Director, I was introduced to a simple but effective way to maximize your efficiency and the efficiency of those in your organization. It can be for members, the leadership team, or even friends looking to keep each accountable. It looks like this:

PROGRAMMING/EVENT CHECKLIST

Name of Event: Art Gallery _ Taft Campus   **Committee:** Isaac
Date: May 18th   **Time:** Afternoon
Location: N/A
Date Contract Received:

✓	Task	Assigned to:	To be completed by:
	General Logistics		
	Reserve space: tables, chairs	Lamarr	3/15
	Materials: canvas holders, tickets		
	Food/Drink: sandwiches, chips/cookies, soda/juice		
	Technology on site		
	Auction		
	Invitation		
	Name tags		
	Guideline/Applications		
	One Month Before Event		
	Design website and RSVP	Amanda	4/19
	Flier for students to sign up / sign up sheet		Done
	Meet with art teachers		Done
	Make announcements in classes starting next week	Amanda	3/22
	Check in with art teachers around student interest	Amanda	3/22
	Two Weeks Before Event		
	One Week Before Event		
	Day of Event		

The powerful part here is an ongoing to-do list, detailing who is accountable to that task, and by when it must be completed. I've recently introduced my students and friends to it (and it's tough to get acclimated if you're not a digital list maker, used to checking a document every day, or writing to do lists, etc.). For me, it's about being accountable for my part, a little bit of competition with my peers, and the ability to hold others accountable to the highest standard of excellence in their work. You can make this an Excel file or there are plenty of apps that allow you to track your workflow.

Monday Morning or Asana are both apps to manage workflow. I find that an Excel spreadsheet is easiest. Ultimately, efficiency and accountability are a choice you make to be excellent in your work and your contributions. In my job as a Dream Director, my administrative consistency has been dramatically heightened and more efficient because of a shared document all Dream Directors have called "dashboards."

Dashboards are meant to give clarity for all members on a team doing the same work so they know what they're accountable for and by when. Typically, it's the same work so there's a level of competition amongst team members (at least for me there is).

The other part of having shared team dashboards is that everyone can hold each other accountable to the highest standard. If you're lagging behind, someone could reach out and see what support you need in order to get back on track. It lends responsibility to everyone on the team to step up, not just the leader of the organization. The reality is that many of the leadership practices we've discussed in this book are about lending leadership, lateral, not top-down type leadership. Here is a sample dashboard:

SAMPLE WORK DASHBOARD

Tasks	Resource/Notes	Due Date	Lamarr	Paula	Nikhita
Attend 3/11 NLD	In person	3/1/2019	Complete	Complete	Complete
Complete weekly Expensify reports	expensify.com	3/11/2019	Complete		Complete
Complete Dreamly entry	dream.ly	3/11/2019	Complete		Complete
Sign up for 1:1 w/ Chief	1:1 Appointment Slot	3/11/2019	Complete	Complete	Complete
Love on Someone else	Yourself		Complete		Complete
Complete TOOL GUIDE	Your own copy of Guide	3/12/2019	Complete		Complete
Share Senior Alumni Enrollment link	godream.org/seniors	3/29/2019	Complete		
Upload Dream Day Consent Forms		3/12/2019	Complete		
Review and mark Innovation Dashboard			Complete		
Love on yourself	Yourself	3/13/2019	Complete		
DISTRIBUTE the Future Summit TFP (Due 3/22)	Final Future Summit Consent Form	3/14/2019	Complete		
DISTRIBUTE the Future Summit COACH (Due 3/22)	Coach Consent Form Future Summit	3/14/2019	Complete		
Attend 3/18 ILD (or if excused, watch the video)	In person	3/14/2019	Complete		
Complete weekly Expensify reports	expensify.com	3/18/2019	Complete		
Complete Dreamly entry	dream.ly	3/18/2019	Complete		
Sign up for 1:1 w/ Chief	1:1 Appointment Slot	3/18/2019	Complete		
Share Tool Guide w/ tester	Your own copy of Guide	3/18/2019	Complete		
Say something positive to yourself in the mirror	Yourself	3/19/2019	Complete		
Write the date when you will TEST	Use this spreadsheet	3/19/2019	On Track		
Review and mark Innovation Dashboard	DDI Innovation Dashboard FY 18/19	3/21/2019	Complete		
Read or watch something inspirational	Yourself	3/22/2019			
COLLECT ALL Future Summit TFPs (Due 3/22)	Final Future Summit Consent Form	3/22/2019			
COLLECT ALL Future Summit COACH (Due 3/22)	Coach Consent Form Future Summit	3/22/2019			
UPLOAD FUTURE SUMMIT CONSENT FORM	Future Summit Consent Form FOLDER	3/25/2019			
Continue to share senior enrollment survey	godream.org/seniors	3/29/2019			
STUDENT OPPORTUNITY: Read through & identify any applicable students attending Future Summit	FUTURE SUMMIT TALENT RECRUITMENT OVERVIEW	3/25/2019			
Complete weekly Expensify reports	expensify.com	3/25/2019			
Complete Dreamly entry	dream.ly	3/25/2019			
Sign up for 1:1 w/ Chief	1:1 Appointment Slot	3/29/2019			
COMPLETE TESTER PORTION		3/27/2019			
Spend quality time in nature	Yourself	3/29/2019			
Review and mark Innovation Dashboard	DDI Innovation Dashboard FY 18/19	3/29/2019			
Share your gratitude with someone	Yourself	3/29/2019			

5.3 Project Building Resources for changing the game for yourself and on your campus

RESOURCES TO MAKE IT HAPPEN

MARKETING

postermywall.com
canva.com
stickermule.com
wackybuttons.com
vistaprint.com
ooshirts.com

BUILDING WEBSITES

godaddy.com
splashthat.com
wordpress.com
squarespace.com

PUBLISHING/ MUSIC

lulu.com
createspace.com
soundcloud.com

VIDEO/ EDITING

TikTok (app)
InShot (app)
vimeo.com
youtube.com

FUNDRAISING

Cash App
Square card reader
PayPal card reader
Venmo cash exchange
gofundme.com
kickstarter.com

Legendary Lesson 6: How to Manage Your Time and Why It's Vital for Mental Health

6.1 How to Develop and Maintain Habits

I think it's fair to say that a majority of the involved student leaders are also high academic performers. Academics and leadership typically go hand-in-hand, but they don't have to. In my experience in developing student leaders in high school, it's wise to have a mix of students among your ranks.

I'm clear that different types of students bring different things to the table. I've got about six academically focused students in my student government. I had about six student leaders that their academics are just as important as their involvement. I had about 10 students that are middle of the road academically and are developing the skills necessary to be great outside the classroom. I'm convinced that students who are college ready and even students who aren't going to college need to be focused on 21st century skills in order to be successful *after* high school.

One of the biggest challenges in the high schools I was a Dream Director at was that students were not taught any discipline around keeping an agenda or a calendar of any sort. Many years ago, when I was in middle school and high school, the schools provided planners for students. These days there are so many ways to track your time and be accountable to your work. The reality is that you have to do what works for you best and you have to know what's most natural for you as well. This does take a level of commitment, mentally and verbally, in order to follow through with your plan and track your work to be as efficient as possible.

A great framework for building new habits or taking away old habits is this graphic from Amber Rae, author of *Choose Wonder Over Worry*. First, you have to care. And you'll care in phases all throughout your life. When I was in middle school I used a planner. In high school, I didn't use one because I just did everything when it was due. In college, I attempted to use one but just found that I had enough time to handle all of my responsibilities without needing to write everything down.

HOW TO RESET HABITS

By: @heyamberrae

HABIT I WANT TO CHANGE:	WHAT IT GIVES ME:	WHAT I CAN REPLACE IT WITH:	SO... I WILL:
Wake up & grab phone	Energy & connection	Journaling & cup of tea	Move phone to other room
Critical self-talk	A sense of control	Humor & detachment	Nickname my critic
Sitting all day	Productivity & flow	Walking meetings	Schedule as such.
Evening Wine	Pleasure & relaxation	Restorative yoga	Schedule 5 classes

Intentionality is also key here. This generation of young people that this book is written for has a long list of distractions that don't always allow you to stay focused. Our phones have become our lives and so much so that things on there can distract us from studying, from listening, from staying focused on what you're trying to accomplish. Intention allows you to clearly determine where you want to focus your energy and put all of your energy into that. Here are a few ways to evaluate your intentions and get in action.

- Aim for short sprints of time instead of lofty long ones; one week instead of a month and build from there.

- Soft Schedule structure where you spend 1-3 hours doing a certain activity with some flexibility.
- Reps in the gym, repeat, repeat, repeat.
- Be open to learning a new way of doing old things.
- Be kind to yourself if you don't get it right every time; it's okay.

6.2 Know your values so you can ALWAYS BE YOURSELF!

I don't want to define what values are for any young person. But, to me, my values are my compass for decision-making, how I spend my time and how I live my life. If you can establish a list of values that are important to you, you should be able to identify within them how you intentionally spend your time.

Your values can and will change throughout your life. Some can and will stay the same as well. I was never asked to identify my values in college. You don't ever have to pretend to be someone you aren't. You have values you live into now; you just don't know that they're called your values and you may not know that they're that important to you (yet). Looking back on when I was in college, I valued:

Then:

- community
- leadership
- socializing/fun
- friendship
- fashion

Now:

- Health/Wellness
- Freedom/Flexibility
- Family/Friendship
- Gratitude
- Personal Growth
- Empathy for others
- Travel Experiences

Throughout my college experience, I ran away from leadership positions but I was still a leader. I ran toward jobs and opportunities that allowed me to do what I do best, which, as you can see in my values list from when I was in college. I did what I wanted to do based on my values, even though I didn't know it then. There is power in knowing who you are and what you want your life to be about. It makes it more difficult to convince you to make bad decisions or feel like you've made wrong ones. It also helps you make decisions faster when you need to. Many of you know who you are but you aren't quite ready to own it. This is why you have to write them down. Now is the time: BE YOU! Your mental wellness will thank you for it.

My point here is that when you know what you value, you know exactly where to spend your time. You can look at your values and say," how do I spend my time falling into any of these areas?" If they don't, there's a good chance you're spending time doing something that doesn't align with your values, which means you probably should stop doing it. Establishing what your values are can also help you in your decision-making process. There will come a point in your college career (or after you graduate high school) when you will have to make a decision about your future.

Which club or organization should I join?

What major should I choose and how?

Go away for college or stay home? How?

What job should I take?

Law school or grad school?

Move internationally or not. Move back home after college or stay where I'm at?

All these decisions can be made slightly easier by looking at your values and using them as a guide for your life decisions. Same way you use your morals to distinguish between right and wrong. It's unspoken, you just know what your morals are. Your values should be just as influential in your life. You should know them, have them written down, keep them close to you and review them often.

So, when a tough decision comes up, and it's bound to happen, you make sound, confident and quick decisions. Of course, there are a lot of variables you'll need to do your homework before you decide, but at the foundation of it, you'll know what you really want to do. It's just fear, uncertainty and insecurity holding you back from doing the thing you know you want to do. I believe the question we all ask ourselves is, "Can I actually do this?" Those things are very real for many of us. But they are typically mental roadblocks, not physical ones holding you back. Yes, you can. So take your time, talk to people in your life you care about, review your values, and decide when you're ready.

So much of this can be solved by accepting that failure is a part of life and we'll talk about that in the next section.

Values can also help you overcome and fight through life challenges because they are another version of discovering your *Why* and knowing your purpose. When you think deeply about why you do things, it can give you a lot of answers but how often do you listen to those answers when you're in the heat of the moment? Especially for things in your life that seem like they have nothing to do with each other.

If you know you value family and they are a *huge* part of why you want to graduate high school, get that GED, go to college, or get that Master's degree, is it so eventually you can support them or help your parents financially? How does sleeping through a class, not getting tutoring when you know you need it or not going the extra mile to get another scholarship help you ultimately fulfill your values, the things that are most important to you? It won't.

VALUES LIST

Choose 5 core values from the following list. Add your own to the list if you choose. Circle your top 5.

• Acceptance	• Freedom	• Purpose
• Adaptability	• Gratitude	• Responsibility
• Awareness	• Happiness	• Service
• Balance	• Health	• Spirituality
• Calmness	• Humility	• Trust
• Community	• Innovation	• Understanding
• Compassion	• Knowledge	• Wealth
• Creativity	• Leadership	• Wisdom
• Discipline	• Love	• Wonder
• Empathy	• Moderation	
• Family	• Peace	

Write your own list of values below:

KNOW YOUR VALUES

Write your own list of values below:

1.   6.

2.   7.

3.   8.

4.   9.

5.   10.

6.3 Facing FEAR and FAILURE

Previously, we started talking about facing failure and how fear and uncertainty can hold you back. Fear is usually a state of mental being. Fear is what you feel when you don't want to disappoint someone. Fear is what you feel when you don't want to share something private. Fear is what you feel when you don't think you're enough or deserving. These are the fears we usually hide and keep deep down. We all have fears and, for many of us, we're also scared of facing failure. And that's fine. That's normal.

I often say that **fear** is a mental state of being instead of something that's actually happening in your real life. Typically, the way fear works is you have one bad experience when you're younger and it prevents you from altering how that experience will go in the future. So, now you're mentally restrained from doing anything because you're traumatized. Trauma shows up in your world typically in these 6 ways after something has happened to you. It takes many forms, including guilt, shame, imperfection, feeling broken, feeling unloved, and feeling blame.

THE SELF-SABOTAGE FORMULA

By: Psychic Life Coach Kailo

GUILT	BLAME	SHAME
Because I carry guilt, therefore: I should be punished	Because I carry blame, therefore: I should carry all blunders	Because I am ashamed, therefore: I should hide/ suppress

UNLOVED	BROKEN	IMPERFECT
Because I am unloved, therefore: I should be perfect	Because I am broken, therefore: I should appear whole	Because I am imperfect, therefore: I should imitate

So, how do you live your life and push through these moments that seem absolutely impossible to move past? I'm not a therapist by any means, but here's some advice:

- Always seek professional therapy or talk to your school counselor to help work through some of these moments that might have happened when you were younger, but still feel so real.
- Seek out life coaching or mentorship, which can help you take more of an actionable approach to overcoming trauma.
- Communicate your feelings to yourself by writing or journaling what's happening in your life and

taking time to reflect on what's going well amongst all the challenges.

- Start to share your story. Share your struggles, challenges and insecurities in everyday conversation to normalize not only sharing the positive things in your life.

One of my favorite movie scenes of all time is from the movie *8 Mile*. The final battle rap scene has Eminem's character B-Rabbit getting ready to battle the main antagonist in the movie, Anthony Mackie's character, Papa-Doc. B-Rabbit gets to rap first. In his freestyle, B-Rabbit becomes a legend himself. His rap consists of reminding Papa-Doc and telling the crowd every single failure, embarrassment, or insecurity that he had throughout the movie. Most of this was caused by Papa Doc and his crew. He ends the rap with, "Here, tell these people something they don't know about me." He throws the microphone over to Papa Doc and when it's his turn to start rapping, he chokes and has nothing to say!

Young people want to hide the things that make you most vulnerable but Legendary Leaders learn to share their vulnerability as inspiration and to be relatable and accessible to those that follow them. If your people know that you have shared experiences (with them), it's easier to build trust and lead them.

Your biggest life challenges are also your greatest strengths. Use them to own your story. Do not let anyone tell your story for you or use it against you to bring you down or make you feel like you aren't enough. When you control the narrative, you leave being a victim to the circumstances to be accountable for what happened and that mindset shift makes a difference in leadership.

If you don't quite need these resources and outlets to overcome your trauma, I'm going to recommend some other mindset tips to push through failure. These were the avenues that I personally chose in my leadership journey to keep my mindset strong and feel like I could never lose.

I want to first introduce you to the idea of progress over perfection. It's impossible to be perfect so stop trying to be.The mental battle against failure begins with the one in your mind. It's you versus you. When you realize that you don't need to be perfect, but you just need to commit to trying to be better than you were yesterday, you can win the mental edge. You'll also know that some days this won't be the case and that's ok, too.

I want to share a framework with you about failure and how to shift your mindset. We must acknowledge that true failure is actually not doing what you wanted and then regretting you didn't. It's only possible to fail if you never try. Trying and it not working out the way you wanted is called giving it a shot. All you can do is try to succeed in a way that makes you feel good about what you're creating, not in comparison to others or their definition of success.

FAIL - FIRST ATTEMPT IN LEARNING

Your first attempt at learning means there's something in you that says, 'Why not me? Why can't I do

this? Why can't I be the one that does this in my family?'
There is some love, support or mentorship that you have or
sought out that doesn't have you stuck or not moving
toward your ambitions. This is huge and you are lucky.
You aren't suffering from self-doubt or a lack of
confidence, even if you're suffering from imposter
syndrome. But hey, we're all imposters at something at
some point in our lives.

The first time you do anything, why would you
expect to be great at it? Why would I expect to crush it?
Not that it's not possible, but more than likely you're not
going to be great at it and all you can do is try again and
ask more questions or get more help. Failing simply gives
you a chance to learn how to make it better *next time*.

The issue here is that your environments don't
really give you space to fail and not feel insecure or feel
bad about yourself. This is why you have to stand up for
yourself, advocate for getting more help, asking specific
questions and opening doors for yourself that maybe other
students wouldn't ask because they're scared or don't know
how.

It doesn't matter if you're taking a test or in the
middle of a project; *always* know what the expectations are
so you can create a plan that allows you to meet or exceed
the expectations and your teacher, leader or advisor should
be able to provide you with a roadmap on how to do that.
So ... *ask*!

SAIL - SECOND ATTEMPT IN LEARNING

The second time you do something, maybe you don't believe you failed the first time or that it was fluke. Or you actually didn't prepare as much as you should have. I see you! It happens to the best of us. I failed once, many times. Know what I asked myself? *How bad do you want it?* Come, try again!

TAIL - THIRD ATTEMPT IN LEARNING

The third time is where you seek support. What can you do differently? Who can help me do it better? Where can I get support? Who has already done this? Can he or she help me do it, too? I'd argue that you could ask these questions before you even *start* to prevent yourself from having to go through some of these aches and pains of failure. Go get help!

One example that really resonates with me is when I was teaching some mindset tricks to fight against **fear** and **failure** to some freshmen. One of the students shared an example of when they had fear. She mentioned that she thought that transitioning from 8th grade to 9th that she wouldn't make or have any friends once she got to high school. The reality was that thinking things weren't going to work out for her before they even happened was dictating her future behavior. The same things can happen to us all.

The subtle mindset shift is instead living in fear and negative energy. Live in possibility by using the word, *maybe*. Instead of saying, 'I'm so scared that I'm not going to have friends next year,' you could say, '*Maybe* I will actually find friends next year.' That student's fear of the unknown didn't end up being her reality. She made plenty of friends and was able to look back and see that her fear was just **f**alse **e**vidence **a**ppearing **r**eal. That's all it is.

The reality is we fail all the time; we just don't call it failure. You wanted to study for the test you have on Friday or Monday, but you didn't. You failed. You wanted to go to the gym four days this week, but you only went twice. You failed. You wanted to call your grandma every weekend for a month and you missed the last week of the month. You failed. The stakes make a difference in what we will look at as greater failures than others, but the reality is you look at all failures as equal then it will help you as a Legendary Leader to move forward faster and on to the next play (to use a sports analogy). The longer you dwell on your failures, the more it prevents you from moving forward. It's okay to spend time figuring out what you did wrong and it's also okay to feel sad or bad about failing. The part you have to avoid is staying there and staying stuck there. Remember to F.A.I.L.: this is your "first attempt at learning"!

6.4 Planners and Calendars

I always found it difficult in high school and college to keep a calendar. It was also that way for many of my student leaders that I've worked with over the last six years in New York City. I cannot stress enough how important it is that you get in the habit of updating your calendar as often as possible.

I would first recommend engaging in your Google Calendar on your phone; it's probably the easiest to get accustomed to. The habit is putting whatever you have agreed to or other commitments in your calendar as soon as you make them. A legend keeps their word. One of the greatest downfalls of young people and student leaders, even the best of them, is being scared to own up to commitments they can't keep. Then what happens is they go silent or they ghost. This is not a quality you want to develop in any life scenario. Legendary Leaders take ownership and responsibility when they can't show up. You should be putting your assignments, student org meetings, classes, times and even time to call your mom in your calendar.

6.5 Learning how to say 'No.'

Earlier in the book we discussed that it's okay to be "off" sometimes. One of the greatest skills legendary leaders need is the ability to say no. They need to recognize when they're doing too much and are overwhelmed. It's okay for legendary leaders to say no, that they don't have the skills or resources to make something happen that someone else might be able to do better.

Saying no is not an admission of not being capable, but actually a recognition of not needing to do everything all the time and wanting to be able to trust in your members and teammates to get work done just as effectively as you might.

Saying no takes practice. Personally, I was so concerned with being nice there wasn't much I would have said no to. When it comes to leadership, as a young person, saying yes to everything doesn't really serve you. The challenge is when you don't learn to say no when you're younger, you certainly aren't going to say no when you're older because it becomes a habit. The more we do, the more it drives habits. The more we don't say 'no' to things we should (or want to) say 'no' to, the more likely we'll keep repeating the pattern..

Do whatever it takes to break the pattern. All these phrases don't leave much room for you to think about doing anything but getting the job done. The reality is the job ain't going anywhere and the work will always need to be done. The question becomes, 'When are you going to take control of it instead of letting it control you?'

The idea of this can seem super uncomfortable for even many professionals. Saying no allows you to establish boundaries of what you're willing to take or not take inside a team environment. Some could look at it as not being a team player, but everyone is entitled to their professional work standards and should not be judged harshly for not doing work that falls outside of their responsibilities. These are the things that companies and managers can take advantage of: Someone who doesn't know how to say no or that is "too nice" could be taken advantage of and not compensated for always going the extra mile for the team.

For our high school friends, particularly from small schools and small communities, they may suffer from this the most. In my experience in speaking around America, our strongest legendary leaders in high schools all over the country have struggled with saying no and advocating for themselves. They feel a lot of pressure to do everything, even when it is no longer interesting to them or something they're passionate about. A lot of this pressure comes from parents, but also a lot of it, I believe, is self-inflicted because young people aren't used to making their own choices, but are more used to being told what they should or shouldn't do. Legendary Leaders need to know what's taking up their time and, more importantly, what's taking up their time that is not allowing them to give their best to the people, teams and organizations that they're a part of.

Below is a time chart for you to complete in order to visualize how you spend your time and what -in your schedule- doesn't allow you to operate at your absolute best. Maybe you're no longer passionate about the organization or sport you're doing. Maybe you need to spend less time on after-school clubs so you can find a job. Whatever it is, it helps to visually see how you are spending your time so you can make decisions and possibly say 'no' if you need to. It takes courage. These are the things that lead young people to be stressed out, get anxiety, and be overwhelmed with their schedules.

ACTIVITY LOG / TIME LOG

ACTIVITY	24 HRS / DAY	168 HRS / WEEK	% OF TIME

TOTALS: # of Activities:

I want every single one of you Legendary Leaders to subscribe to the Drop Something Method. After you do this activity, I want you to look at your schedule and look at one of two things:

1) What could you drop from your schedule that would free up time to do something you enjoy or to give you more free time?

2) What could you drop that you no longer care about or are passionate about?

I remember vividly when I was a sophomore in high school and no longer wanted to be in Jr. ROTC. It was a conversation I wasn't sure how it would go. My dad was military, I was raised in a military family, but it was clear early on that the military, though it can provide a wonderful life, wasn't for me! When I realized I wanted to tell my parents so I could just transfer into a gym class (which was a joke, lol), I mustered up the courage to talk to them. One day, my parents and I were driving to the mall one weekend and I just said it. "I don't want to do ROTC anymore." And both my parents just said, "Ok!" That was the end of it. There was no pressure, no attempt to make me feel guilty. There was no expectation attached to it for them. It all came from me.

We do this to ourselves a lot and it forces us to stay in things we truly don't care for anymore. Sometimes we submit to parents and teachers because we assume they know what's right for us. Sometimes you do know what's right for you and you have to speak up for yourself.

6.5 How to Ask for Help

I don't want to feel dumb.

I don't want to look stupid.

Nobody will understand what I'm going through.

I can't believe I have to do all of this.

I can't handle all this on my own.

I can just do it better.

Let me know if I can try it on my own first.

I am strong, independent and I don't need anyone, too much pride.

These are some thoughts that go through our minds when we need help but are scared to ask for it. Many of us really operate from a place of coping even when we think that we're being open and asking for help. The reality is, it's hard to ask for help. It's hard to admit, especially when you're the leader or the student that always "gets" it that you don't understand something or you need support in order to complete a project.

Mentorship is a great way to solve the 'asking for help' problem. For me, personally, it has always been a struggle for me and it received mentorship and support mainly because my ego was too big. Many years ago, when I first started my speaking business, I was doing some workshops for 100 black men and I was approached by one of the officers in the group about helping make my business better. For some reason there was something he said that struck me the wrong way and I've had a negative opinion about mentorship since.

Fast forward 10 years and it took many years of being stagnant and not gaining the opportunities I believed I deserved to finally stop and ask for help. That help came in the form of Carlos Ojeda Jr. who has also contributed to my speaking career in a way that is helpful and allows me to trust that he'll be there. He has given to me and I haven given to him.

Acknowledge to yourself that you need help and find someone who has done what you want to do and have them help you find a coach or mentor. Legendary Leaders are the *first* to know they can't do everything and, more importantly, they do not need to do or know everything. It's a myth. Utilize your team and network.

All of the major moments of growth I made in my life I did with the support and help of a mentor or a coach. Throughout my adulthood, I've struggled with gaining and losing weight. I had high blood pressure. I've felt insecure about my body. I was not seeing any progress and it was difficult for me to have the discipline needed to see the results I wanted to see. I hired my friend and personal trainer, Chet Fortune, on multiple occasions to help achieve results I couldn't achieve on my own.

From the time I was 14 until I was 32, I had challenges with building a relationship with my father because of things that happened between my parents when I was younger. Our lack of relationship really sat on me and I held onto it for years. I didn't learn how to overcome trauma until I paid to go to a life coaching workshop that helped me communicate with my father about how I'd been feeling for 18 years. I'm not sure if I ever would have had the courage to do it on my own.

I did it with help.

What is Legendary is failing, being scared to do something, not knowing how to do something and then telling the story about how you overcame it so you can inspire and convince someone else that if you could do it they can do it.

The reality about asking for help is **you have to be ready.** This process can take a while and this is why it's important for you to acknowledge (in your head, in your journal, in your conversations with your friends... wherever you can or need to) that you might need help. Then, when you're ready, you make the ask.

Chapter 7: Legendary Leaders

When I'm speaking around the country, I love getting to share stories of students that I've worked with over the years to give you all some motivation. These leaders are some of the best of the best in the country. They are definitely some of the best students I've ever worked with. The students on the cover of this book are special young people and they deserve to have their story told.

Rosie M.

I met Rosie when she was a Junior at Bronx Collegiate Academy. She was a smart student and involved with the student government. She was an extremely hard worker. Not knowing Rosie, that is what I noticed about her. She just outworked everyone else and that's what made her great.

Rosie was also shy and passive. I knew that by the end I wanted to develop Rosie so she could have more authority and take charge. The importance of this was ultimately to get her to find her voice, which she'll always have for the rest of her life. She ended up co-creating a freshman mentoring program to help freshmen get acquainted with life in high school. She was a great leader and someone that the entire school could look up to.

Rosie now has a Bachelor's degree in Psychology from Pace University in New York City. She is preparing to start her Master's degree in the fall!

Aminata N.

I also met Aminata when she was a junior in high school at Bronx Collegiate Academy. She was a French born African descent multilingual student with a work ethic like you wouldn't believe. Aminata and Rosie were both students who knew who they were and really leaned into that. It's not every day you meet high school students this mature and ready to take on (literally) any task. She was one of the few main students in the student government and was academically sound.

Aminata always knew that academics wasn't the only thing that was going to get her into and through college. She needed soft skills and her senior year she took off! She helped lead our back-to-school event, co-founded the BCA mentoring program and spent time meeting professionals in her field to learn more directly from anthropologists. Aminata is now a graduate from the University of Albany with a degree in Psychology. She is my mentee and someone I know will be changing the world for the better! She now works as the Community Prosecution Coordinator at the City of Albany, NY District Attorney's office.

Gissell J.

I met Gissell when she was a Sophomore in High school. When I met her, she was immediately interested in being part of the Dream Team that I was building at The College Academy. Gissell was a strong student academically and she would often tell me that she was going to go to college for Nursing. The more conversations I had with Gissell, the more I became aware that she actually didn't want to do nursing. She would constantly be talking about fashion, fashion shows, photography and modeling. At some point, she knew she had to speak with her mom because mom was in the fashion industry and frankly knows how challenging it can be to be successful.

Her mom always just wanted her to *not* have the same struggles in the fashion industry she had, so she wanted her to be a nurse. The reality was that Gissell wasn't passionate about nursing, but she was about fashion. She went on to put on three fashion shows in our school her last two years of high school. She also co-hosted a fashion show in NYC where she debuted her first five designs, including her own prom dress that she designed and crafted herself.

She went on to graduate as the salutatorian from her high school and ended up getting a full ride scholarship to Cazenovia College. She graduated with a degree in Fashion Merchandising and Fashion Design. She, too, has earned a Master's degree in her field and now works on 5th Avenue in NYC living out her passion for fashion.

Arkey B.

I met the one and the only Arkey during his junior year of high school. Before I moved to NYC to work at The College Academy in Washington Heights, I heard stories of a kid who wanted to go to Princeton so badly that he raised over $2,000 from classmates, friends and staff to go there for a summer program. By the time I arrived at the beginning of his junior year, I seeked him out immediately.

He called me Big D.I.P. = Dreams, Inspiration and Passion. That's what students called my room. Arkey was one of the first students to work with me to create a passion project. Arkey wanted to start a tutoring program from freshman and sophomore students in math and science to help prepare them for college. He called it the Successful Struggle. What I didn't tell you is that Arkey was displaced and wasn't in school from 6th through 9th grade. He also wasn't in school. He jumped around from foster care to group homes to close family. Arkey was truly a Legendary Leader because he had a calling.

Everyday he operated with an intense purpose to help all students focus on their education and get admitted into college. He ended up graduating as the valedictorian of his school and went to one of the top liberal arts colleges in the country, Williams College, to get a degree in Economics. After that, he was admitted to Yale University to get his Master's degree. Two summers ago Arkey called me and said, "Lamarr, I'm going blue." I said, "You joined a gang? What do you mean?"

He said, " I got admitted into the University of Michigan to get my PhD in Economics!" From homeless to Phd; if he can do it, you can do it as well!

Theo B.

In 2016, I had an opportunity to speak at a student leadership conference in upstate New York in central square high school. My flight to the event had been canceled the night prior and I was instructed to call the president of the student council, Theo Burtis. He got me squared away and created a new plan without me to his advisor and I was thoroughly impressed.

The next day I arrived at the event late to give the afternoon keynote instead of the morning keynote. I also watched Theo and his team run a master class on how students can lead. Theo and I have been linked ever since.

Two years ago, he called me up asking for mentorship so he could learn the ropes of what it would take to become a motivational speaker. Six months after that he called me again with a problem for us to solve. For the last year and a half we've been building a journal together for young adults aged 17-22 to help them stand strong against anxiety, stress, feeling lonely and low self-esteem.

Amada A.

Every educator has one student that actually is impacted by them because they display what it means to soak everything in and learn what it takes to be the greatest version of themselves. Amada is that student for me.

When I first met Amada, she was a sophomore in high school. She wanted to do photography so I gave her and another student the opportunity to take photos for an event. She even wrote a grant to get a brand new camera. By the end of the year, she was already over photography. The next year, Amada decided she wanted to be the best leader of our student government that she could be.

She led meetings, led her own project, and supported and coached other students to become stronger leaders. Amada always asked me questions about what it took to be better and she really wanted to be great academically and leadership-wise. Her senior year - although she didn't love art and photography anymore- she created a campus wide art show for passionate artists on the entire campus, and it was a huge success. She's now a senior in college majoring in hospitality management. Amada is like a little sister to me. Her and her mother have become very close family friends and I'm incredibly proud of the young woman she is becoming.

Victoria D.

I met Victoria at the NYSCYLA state conference in 2016 and was quickly connected to her and the student government leaders at Somers High School! At the time, Victoria was the student body president of her high school and the New York State student body President as well. I've always been mesmerized by how students do this. Legitimately, students are by far the busiest people in our society, having to balance so many aspects of life.

Victoria was one of those students. The reality is that some students got it and some students don't. Vic hosted me as a speaker at her school and pretty much organized the whole day along with her advisor and my friend Brenda O'Shea.

She recently graduated from Stony Brook College on Long Island and has contributed to a number of projects I've worked on to benefit college students. She now attends Emory University in Atlanta, getting her Master's degree in Public Health. She plans to go to medical school once she completes her Master's degree!

Kingsley B. and Yondez W.

In 2019, I traveled to Berea, Kentucky to speak at Berea College. Berea is unique because it's one of the few tuition-free schools where every student on campus has a full ride scholarship and is also given a job as part of the requirements to attend the university. I was speaking to the freshmen class who are required to attend programming once a month. I was speaking to them about how to find their passion.

At the end of the event, Kingsley approached me and started asking questions about what I do and he expressed that he likes to do similar work. By the end of our conversation, he asked me if he and his close friend Yondez, who was not at the event, could come to New York over their spring break and do work with my student leaders! Talk about Legendary! A month and a half later they arrived in NYC and crashed on my couches for three days and spent two days with me building a workshop for my student leaders around discovering their values.

I was so incredibly impressed with these two young men and they truly left an impression on me. They both ended up leaving Berea before graduating. They are now following their passions and continue to learn and explore what life has to offer them. Yondez moved to LA and does a number of jobs that fill his passion cup. Kingsley lives in Virginia and spreads the gospel of the Lord!

Conclusion - Be Legendary!

There were a lot of legendary tips in this book about how to become LEGENDARY before, after and during college. *But,* through all those tips and gems the one thing I want you to leave with what it means to be LEGENDARY is simply ***being good to people in life***! Nothing more and nothing less.

Love for others.

Look out for others.

Know others a little deeper than you normally would.

Know yourself.

Ask questions about their wants, needs and desires.

Ask for help.

Give them the freedom to be who they are and to show their talents and abilities.

Don't judge their life, especially if you don't know where they've been.

So much of the advice given in these pages requires you to take a hard look at yourself and decide how you want to leave people as a boss, a peer, a leader, a friend, a family member, a co-worker and, more importantly, as a human being.

Legendary leaders are those that lift others up at all cost and are willing to always look at themselves in the mirror to see how they can be better than they were yesterday, which is the hardest part.

Be Legendary my friends. I love you all and I hope you've enjoyed this read!

About the Author

Nationally recognized Youth Speaker, Executive Coach, Leadership Expert and Podcast Host, Lamarr Womble helps audiences in accessing a more fulfilled life by helping you discover it's not just about what you do but who you want to be. On the journey to becoming the greatest version of yourself, it's essential that you:

- Conquer the battle in your mind
- Do work you love
- Lead self/others to happiness

These are the key components to you winning and living a powerful life! Lamarr has delivered and coached this message to over 60,000 students, educators and corporate professionals since 2008.

Lamarr has been:

- Featured as a TEDx and TEDx Youth Speaker

- Featured on MSNBC.com

- The Co-Host of The Men Up Up Podcast | www.themenup.com

- The author of The You Book Journal, The Passion Workbook and The Skills Frameworks for Legendary Leaders | www.passionforleadership.com

- An Executive Leadership and Life Coach | www.lamarrwomble.com

Made in the USA
Monee, IL
20 January 2026

41215031R00075